THE COMPLETE
SOUS VIDE COOKBOOK

200+ RECIPES TO COOK AT HOME LIKE A CHEF

Written by: Martha Scott

Warning-Disclaimer

Contents

INTRODUCTION

Are you ready to take your cooking to the next level? Do you want to learn advanced techniques, develop new culinary skills, and impress your foodiest friends? What if somebody told you that you could reveal the secret weapon of world's top chefs?

Take on a fresh challenge with this cookbook and try a sous vide method. A perfect salmon steak. A juicy and tender chicken that melts on your tongue. A saucy, deli-style meat without excess oil – you can have a food that's perfectly cooked immediately using the sous vide method of cooking. Maybe you have been misled by this fancy French name, so take the step back. Believe or not, you can implement this technique in your kitchen and cook restaurant-style meals immediately.

Sous vide is the process of cooking food at a precisely controlled temperature and time; your food should be cooked at the temperature it will be served at. Put simply, this method involves putting food in a vacuum seal bags and cooking it in a specially designed water bath.

A definition of sous vide according to Wikipedia is: "Sous-vide (/su: vi: d/; French for "under vacuum') is a method of cooking in which food is placed in a plastic pouch or a glass jar and then placed in a water bath or steam environment for longer than normal cooking times (usually 1 to 7 hours, up to 48 or more in some cases) at an accurately regulated temperature."

If you follow particular rules, you will have perfectly cooked and well-balanced meals, time and time again. You will achieve better nutrition, richer flavors and more authentic appearance of your food than never before with conventional cooking methods.

Getting Started: How it Works?

The whole cooking process in a sous vide device is easy to follow. Regardless of this simplicity, there are essential things you need to know to get started.

1. **Safety reasons**
   - First things first: never use a sous vide equipment until you have read the manufacturer's manual for operation and cleaning! "Preparation is half the battle"; it might sound like a cliché, but this is so true. If you are new to the sous vide, it is imperative to read instructional guides provided by the manufacturer. On the other hand, if you are familiar with this cooking method, you still need to consult the manual on a regular basis.
   - Learn basic steps to food safety to reduce the risk of individuals becoming sick from foodborne illnesses. It is strongly recommended to consult sous vide temperature chart for any type of food. It's imperative that a cooking pouch is fully submerged in hot water for the entire duration of cooking; it will significantly reduce any risk of bacterial growth. Although this is a common and understandable concern, it is no more dangerous to you than any other cooking method.
   - Always cover the water bath with a lid or a piece of foil to minimize evaporation.
   - As a precaution in case something happens, you should check the cooking process every few hours. For instance, the cooking pouch isn't fully immersed so you should reseal it or add weights to the top.

2. **Essential kitchen equipment – must haves**
   Chefs and food experts have used the sous vide cooking in professional kitchens for decades, but their equipment is bulky and expensive. The growing awareness of healthy eating habits encourages manufacturers to produce home devices that are available, inexpensive and practical. Luckily, you do not need a lot of fancy gear to cook in this way. There are many items available to you and some of them you probably already have in your kitchen. You will need the following tools:
   - An immersion circulator.
   - A water bath – feel free to use any size of pot that you already have.
   - Vacuum seal bags and resealable jars that are certified by their manufacturers as suitable for sous vide cooking.
   - Cooking utensils such as tongs, spoons, and skimmers.

   In addition, you will need a cast-iron skillet or a kitchen blowtorch to finish your meals like a Michelin-starred chef. A small propane gas torch does wonders for your sous vide meals. Once you gather this basic equipment, it's time to get cooking!

3. **Time and temperature guide**

When it comes to the cooking, the temperature is one of the most important things that we need to know. It can turn your food from ordinary meal into the real piece of art. The key to the successful sous vide cooking is consistent heat, a precise temperature control. It means that you can achieve perfectly predictable results without much hassle and a particular culinary training.

Take a steak (ribeye, porterhouse or T-bone) as an example. If you like rare steak, the ideal temperature will be between 120 and 138 degrees F. If you like medium-rare steak, you should set your sous vide machine from 129 to 134 degrees F. Then, if you prefer medium steak, you should use 135 to 144 degrees F.

Time is also essential component of successful sous vide cooking. When it comes to the timing range, make sure that the food you prepare with sous vide is as safe as possible. That's why steaks (one-inch thick or less), that are cooked under 130 degrees F, should not be cooked longer than two and a half hours.

Contrary to what you might think, cooking with extreme precision is your success formula. To sum up, you should use a time and temperature guide that is reliable and contain all of the information you need to cook your food sous vide.

4. **What is the secret behind sous vide cooking?**

When using conventional cooking methods such as grilling, roasting, sautéing, and frying, the moisture of your food is constantly evaporating into the surrounding water or air. On the other hand, vacuum sealing prevents a loss of nutrients and moisture. A cooking pouch protects your food from direct contact with water, which results in food that is perfectly cooked every time.

When you cook meat sous vide, the connective tissues are broken down but it still keeps your food moist and juicy. It can break down collagen and tenderize tougher cuts but the meat still has its moisture and stays pink in the middle. Even the most delicate piece of fish cooks perfectly in this way. Further, sous vide prevents your favorite veggies to end up dull and mushy because they still have their bright colors and just the right crunchiness.

Sous vide has proven to be the great kitchen technique of those home cooks who don't want to spend all day in the kitchen but want to offer five-star meals to their families.

Why Is Sous Vide Good For You?

1. **Opt for convenience by choosing the right cooking method.**

   On the surface, this cooking method might seem complicated but it is not difficult at all. While there are variations within each recipe, generally, you should follow a few simple steps:

   1) flavor your food; 2) put the ingredients into a cooking pouch and seal it tightly; 3) submerge the cooking pouches in the preheated water bath; 4) set the temperature and let it simmer for a particular amount of time. Meanwhile, you can pour yourself a glass of wine and let the sous vide device do the rest; 5) afterwards, in order to get a great flavor and appearance, especially for meat, you should quickly sear or brown food in a skillet or using a blow torch.

   There are sous vide recipes that call for other methods of finishing your meal; thus, feel free to experiment and make the most out of this extraordinary cooking technique. You can finish your meal on the grill, in a saucepan or grill pan, under the broiler, and so forth. This "intricate appliance" does an amazing job for you!

2. **Your health is a top-priority.**

   There is no doubt that home-cooked meals are healthier than processed foods. When cooking food in a vacuum seal pouch, you can "lock in" all flavors and vitamins. In addition, removing the air will prevent food from oxidizing and turn your boring meals into eye-catching, nutritious and flavorful creations.

   Normally, foods are cooked in water or lots of oil. When you cook food sous vide, you don't have to use additional oil or another unhealthy flavor "enhancer". With sous vide, foods are easier to digest because of the long cooking time.

   When all is said and done, cooking food at home means you have control over ingredients, calories and nutrition, while providing better-tasting food.

3. **Hands-off cooking will save you tons of time.**

   Generally speaking, we are constantly on the hunt for new intelligent solutions to improve the quality of our lives. In addition to providing an extremely tasty food, sous vide can save your time in the kitchen. You can plan ahead by cooking double batches of meat and vegetables, and then, freeze a large amount of food for a busy week. Sous vide will help you to get organized by making go-to quick meals with basic ingredients. It also allows flexibility with the cooking times so food is brought to the optimum temperature and is held at this temperature over an extensive duration of time. You just need to set up your device and go about your business.

This cooking method allows you to cook multiple meals at once. Simultaneously and successfully! Here is a time-saving tip: keep basic ingredients such as garlic, onion, chili peppers, and your favorite spice combos on hand as they add a little something extra to every sous vide dish. This is also a clever space-saving item because you will be able to prepare multiple meals in just one kitchen appliance.

Unlike traditional methods of cooking, you don't need to stand by the stove, stirring your meals, because keeping your food from sticking to the pan is not an issue. Enjoy all the benefits of hands-off cooking and adjust your cooking to your schedule!

4. **Save lots of money in the long-term**
The sous vide technique cooks budget-friendly dishes to perfection. Many of these sous vide recipes call for staples you already have in your pantry. You can choose inexpensive, tougher and fattier cuts of meat. You can save your money by choosing the recipes that call for inexpensive and "less desirable" food such as rice, firm fruit, and so on.

Sous vide device perfectly cooks larger pieces of meat, which makes it an incredible way to save time and money when you cook at home. For instance, you can purchase a whole chicken instead of chicken drumsticks or fillet, or opt for a pork shoulder rather than chops.

Sous vide allows you to cook multiple meals at once, and then, place your food in containers; therefore, you can refrigerate or freeze your food to save for use later, reducing food waste and spoilage.

Six Smart Sous Vide Tricks
That Make Everything Taste Better

For maximum success with sous vide, below are a few hacks to keep in mind.

1. For the best results, before sous vide cooking, meat should be taken out of the refrigerator to sit for 20 to 30 minutes at room temperature. For the same reason, eggs should be at room temperature before sous vide cooking.

2. Avoid adding too many aromatics to your food. Further, you should carefully select the seasonings because they cook with other ingredients for a longer period, intensifying the flavor of your food. If you added too much garlic or strong-flavored herbs such as thyme, rosemary, winter savory, mint or sage, you'll end up with a ruined meal.

3. When dealing with ingredients, don't put too many foods into one cooking pouch at a time; of course, it depends on the size of your pouch. Generally speaking, make sure that the vacuum seal is tight enough so there are no gaps between ingredients and the cooking pouch.

4. For even better results, use two temperature settings with your sous vide device. Initially, cook the meat such as beef, lamb or pork at 120 degrees F for 7 to 8 hours; it will break down the connective tissue so the meat will become softer than usual. After that, increase the heat to the target temperature for the remainder of the cooking time.

5. It's imperative to finish your food in a proper way. For instance, you will need an extremely hot skillet to sear your meal quickly. Make sure to pat dry meat before searing, browning or grilling.

6. To avoid waiting for the water to reach the target temperature, which can take hours, you can bring the water to a boil in a regular pot. You will save your time significantly and help your sous vide device to work better.

A Word about Our Recipe Collection

Flavorful soups, hearty stews, luxurious desserts, deliciously gooey treats, slurp-worthy sauces... If you are desirous of old-fashioned meals to warm your soul, sous vide is your first choice. We have got 215 sous vide recipes ahead: from meat to seafood, from vegan recipes to snacks and appetizers.

Everyone who is lucky enough to own a sous vide device will enjoy this recipe collection. Likewise, everyone who is planning to purchase a sous vide equipment can seize the opportunity to get knowledge about sous vide cooking and its advantages. These recipes will help you to avoid many of the common pitfalls that beginners often encounter. You will find many tips for optimizing your cooking skills and learning to cook like a pro. What inspired you to cook homemade meals? Love, health, gratitude, imagination?

If you're thinking about making the leap from good to great, from average to outstanding, you should embrace over-the-top cooking trends. This nifty kitchen device cooks perfect family meals with more flavor and nutrients than you can imagine!

If you are just afraid of a flop, this cookbook is ready to be your steady kitchen companion and make your cooking experience more enjoyable! These recipes use the ingredients that you most likely already have in your kitchen.

Every recipe includes the list of ingredients, step-by-step directions, cooking time, the number of servings, and nutritional information. Nutrition information will help you to make your dishes healthier and well-balanced, by telling you about ingredients in your recipes. The cookbook is also chock-full of great tips such as substitutions, serving ideas, and so forth.

Go with the flow and experiment with new cooking trends. As you get more comfortable with sous vide cooking, you'll master completely new skills and be able to adapt any traditional recipe to use with this outstanding kitchen device. Simply consult the cooking time chart and try to use ingredients that have similar cooking times if possible.

Forget the dried out, dull food, and indulge in juicy and succulent meats, toothsome and crunchy vegetables, perfectly soft eggs, silken and sophisticated fish, gooey and delectable desserts! Bon appétit!

CHICKEN

1. Sichuan-Style Chicken Legs
(Ready in about 2 hours 15 minutes | Servings 4)

You can use any type of a high-smoke-point oil like grapeseed oil or lard but peanut oil will add a great, unique flavor.
Per serving: 527 Calories; 32.8g Fat; 28.4g Carbs; 27.5g Protein; 2.9g Sugars

Ingredients

4 chicken legs quarters
1 teaspoon sea salt
1/2 teaspoon ground black pepper, or more to taste
1/2 teaspoon smoked cayenne pepper
1 teaspoon dried rosemary
1 teaspoon dried marjoram

1/2 teaspoon mustard seeds
2 tablespoons peanut oil
2 ½ tablespoons soy sauce
2 tablespoons sake
1/2 cup dry-roasted peanuts, unsalted
2 cups cooked long-grain rice, hot

Directions

- Preheat a sous vide water bath to 167 degrees F.
- Rinse the chicken legs; pat them dry. Season the chicken legs with sea salt, black pepper, cayenne pepper, dried rosemary, marjoram, and mustard seeds.
- Place the chicken legs in cooking pouches and seal them tightly.
- Now, submerge the cooking pouches in the water bath; let it simmer for 2 hours. Remove the chicken legs from the cooking pouches.
- Reserve the cooking liquid.
- While the chicken legs rest, preheat a frying pan over medium-high heat. Heat peanut oil.
- Sear the chicken legs, adding the soy sauce and sake, until they are golden brown on all sides; add a splash of cooking liquid as needed.
- Add dry-roasted peanuts and cook an additional minute. Serve garnished with hot rice.

---

2. Paprika Chicken with Artichokes
(Ready in about 1 hour 15 minutes | Servings 4)

Here is a classic family recipe that you can prepare for any occasion! Paprika and sautéed aromatic garlic push this recipe over the edge.
Per serving: 271 Calories; 11.5g Fat; 6.9g Carbs; 34.5g Protein; 0.6g Sugars

Ingredients

3 chicken breast halves, boneless and skinless
1/2 teaspoon sea salt
1/4 teaspoon ground black pepper, or more to taste
1 teaspoon paprika

2 tablespoons olive oil
2 cloves garlic, peeled and minced
1 can (14-ounce) artichoke hearts, quartered

Directions

- Preheat a sous vide water bath to 146 degrees F.
- Season the chicken breast halves with sea salt, black pepper, and paprika.
- Place the seasoned chicken breasts in cooking pouches and seal them tightly. Submerge the cooking pouches in the water bath; cook for 1 hour.
- Remove the chicken breasts from the cooking pouches; pat them dry; reserve the cooking liquid.
- Now, heat 1 tablespoon of olive oil in a pan that is preheated over a medium-high heat. Sear the chicken until it's a light golden brown. Reserve.
- Heat the remaining tablespoon of olive oil. Sauté the garlic until it's aromatic. Add the artichokes; let it simmer for another 8 to 10 minutes, adding the reserved cooking liquid as needed.
- Add the reserved chicken breasts and serve immediately. Bon appétit!

3. Ethiopian-Style Berbere Chicken
(Ready in about 1 hour 10 minutes | Servings 4)

Serve on a bed of lettuce with horseradish mayo, artisanal bread, and vine-ripened tomatoes. It goes perfectly with Ethiopian lentils too.
Per serving: 330 Calories; 21.7g Fat; 19.6g Carbs; 14.2g Protein; 1.2g Sugars

Ingredients

1 pound chicken white meat, bone-in, skin-on and fat trimmed

2 tablespoons Berbere spice mix

1/2 teaspoon celery salt

1/4 teaspoon ground black pepper

1/2 teaspoon celery seeds

2 tablespoons fresh parsley, chopped

1 teaspoon dried onion flakes

1 tablespoon olive oil

Directions

- Preheat a sous vide water bath to 149 degrees F.
- Season the chicken with Berbere spice mix, celery salt, black pepper, celery seeds, parsley, and dried onion flakes.
- Add the chicken to cooking pouches; seal them tightly. Submerge the cooking pouches in the water bath; cook for 1 hour.
- Remove the chicken from the cooking pouches and pat it dry.
- Heat the oil in a skillet that is preheated over a medium-high heat. Once hot, place sous vide chicken skin side down and sear until is crispy.
- Turn over and cook for a further 3 minutes. Serve and enjoy!

---

4. Festive Chicken Salad
(Ready in about 5 hours 35 minutes | Servings 4)

A homemade broth makes everything better. Reserve the broth after cooking and store in your refrigerator for 3 days or freeze for later use. You can pour the broth into the ice cube trays and add these cubes to your favorite soups and stews.
Per serving: 227 Calories; 10.5g Fat; 2.9g Carbs; 28.6g Protein; 1.1g Sugars

Ingredients

1 whole (3 ½ -pound) chicken, bone-in, cut into pieces

1 cup water

2 ½ cups stock, preferably homemade

1 tablespoon Worcestershire sauce

2 sprigs rosemary

1/3 cup dill fronds

1 teaspoon black peppercorns

1 cup celery with leaves, diced into large pieces

4 scallions, trimmed and thinly sliced

2 tablespoons parsley, chopped

1/2 cup mayonnaise

1 teaspoon freshly squeezed lemon juice

1 tablespoon Dijon mustard

Diamond Crystal salt, to taste

Directions

- Preheat a sous vide water bath to 149 degrees F.
- Add the chicken, water, stock, Worcestershire sauce, rosemary, dill, black peppercorns, and celery to cooking pouches and seal them tightly.
- Submerge the cooking pouches in the water bath; cook for 5 hours.
- Next, allow the chicken to cool in the liquid for 30 minutes. Transfer the chicken to a cutting board. Cut chicken crosswise into thin slices.
- Toss the chicken slices with other ingredients in a salad bowl. Serve well chilled.

5. Crispy Chicken Drumettes
(Ready in about 5 hours 15 minutes | Servings 4)

This is a kid-friendly recipe as well as a picnic favorite. It is delicious either hot or cold.
Per serving: 615 Calories; 35.4g Fat; 25.4g Carbs; 46.4g Protein; 0.9g Sugars

Ingredients

4 chicken drumettes
Sea salt and ground black pepper, to your liking
1 teaspoon cayenne pepper
1 egg, well whisked
1 cup all-purpose flour
1/2 teaspoon shallot powder

1/2 teaspoon garlic powder
1/2 teaspoon fennel seeds
1/4 teaspoon allspice
1/4 teaspoon ground bay leaf
Oil for deep-fat frying

Directions

- Preheat a sous vide water bath to 165 degrees F. Rinse the chicken drumettes and pat dry.
- Season the chicken drumettes with salt, black pepper, and cayenne pepper. Place the chicken in cooking pouches and seal them tightly.
- Submerge the cooking pouches in the water bath; cook for 5 hours.
- Meanwhile, prepare a breading station. Beat the egg in a shallow bowl. Mix the flour with the shallot powder, garlic powder, fennel seeds, allspice, and ground bay leaf in another shallow bowl.
- Dredge the chicken drumettes in the whisked egg, then in the seasonings/flour mixture.
- In a deep-fat fryer, heat oil to 360 degrees F. Fry sous vide chicken approximately 5 minutes on each side or until golden brown. Drain on paper towels and serve warm. Bon appétit!

6. Golden Chicken Legs with Horseradish Sauce
(Ready in about 3 hours 10 minutes | Servings 4)

This recipe is perfect for anyone bored of classic chicken meals. It features crispy chicken legs with a creamy, sour and tangy sauce.
Per serving: 466 Calories; 24.3g Fat; 6.1g Carbs; 53.1g Protein; 1.3g Sugars

Ingredients

4 skinless chicken legs, bone in
1/2 teaspoon kosher salt
1/2 teaspoon smoked cayenne pepper
1/2 teaspoon freshly ground black pepper
2 tablespoons olive oil

For the Horseradish Sauce:
1/4 cup fresh horseradish, grated
1 cup sour cream
1 tablespoon Dijon mustard
1 teaspoon white wine vinegar
Salt and black pepper, to taste

Directions

- Preheat a sous vide water bath to 165 degrees F.
- Rinse the chicken legs; pat them dry. Season the chicken legs with sea salt, cayenne pepper, and black pepper.
- Place the chicken legs in cooking pouches and seal them tightly. Now, submerge the cooking pouches in the water bath; let it simmer for 3 hours.
- Remove the chicken legs from the cooking pouches, reserving the cooking liquid.
- Then, add the olive oil to a frying pan and heat on high until it just begins to smoke. Sear the chicken legs approximately 30 seconds per side or until the skin is golden brown and crisp.
- Meanwhile, whisk all of the ingredients for the sauce in a medium mixing bowl; mix until the sauce is smooth and uniform.
- Serve warm chicken legs with the horseradish sauce on the side. Bon appétit!

7. Pineapple Glazed Chicken Tenders
(Ready in about 1 hour 50 minutes | Servings 6)

The honey-pineapple sauce is a quick way to jazz up ordinary chicken tenderloins.
Cook's note: Lard is the perfect shortening in this recipe because it has a high smoke point.
Per serving: 254 Calories; 6.2g Fat; 17.7g Carbs; 31.1g Protein; 16.5g Sugars

Ingredients

2 pounds chicken tenderloins
Sea salt and ground black pepper, to taste
3/4 cup pineapple juice
1/4 cup honey
I teaspoon chipotle powder

1 teaspoon garlic powder
1/2 teaspoon onion powder
3 tablespoons dark rum
1 tablespoon lard, at room temperature

Directions

- Preheat a sous vide water bath to 150 degrees F. Rinse the chicken and pat it dry.
- Season the chicken with salt and black pepper to taste. Place the chicken in cooking pouches and seal them tightly.
- Submerge the cooking pouches in the water bath; cook for 1 hour 40 minutes. Remove the chicken from the cooking pouches, reserving the cooking liquid.
- Combine pineapple juice, honey, chipotle powder, garlic powder, and onion powder in a pan over a moderate heat; cook until the sauce has thickened; remove from heat.
- Now, add dark rum and stir to combine.
- Melt the lard in a pan that is preheated over medium-high heat. Sear the chicken tenderloins for 1 to 2 minutes per side.
- Add the prepared sauce and serve warm. Bon appétit!

---

8. Garlicky Chicken Drumsticks with Bell Peppers
(Ready in about 3 hours 10 minutes | Servings 5)

It's tough to beat juicy chicken drumsticks topped with garlic paste and cooked with fresh peppers. Enjoy!
Per serving: 282 Calories; 16.3g Fat; 8.8g Carbs; 25.3g Protein; 1.4g Sugars

Ingredients

5 chicken drumsticks, bone-in, skin-on
Salt and ground black pepper, to taste
1/4 teaspoon dried marjoram
1/2 teaspoon lemon thyme
1/2 teaspoon fennel seeds

1 tablespoon garlic paste
1 teaspoon grapeseed oil
1 jar (8.5-ounce) sun-dried tomatoes, in oil
2 red bell pepper, deveined and thinly sliced
1 serrano pepper, deveined and thinly sliced

Directions

- Preheat a sous vide water bath to 167 degrees F.
- Season the chicken drumsticks with sea salt, black pepper, marjoram, lemon thyme, and fennel seeds. Now, spread the chicken drumsticks with garlic paste
- Place the chicken drumsticks in cooking pouches and seal them tightly.
- Now, submerge the cooking pouches in the water bath; let it simmer for 3 hours. Remove the chicken drumsticks from the cooking pouches.
- Heat the oil in a nonstick skillet over medium-high heat. Sear the chicken for 1 minute on each side; reserve. Add sun-dried tomatoes, along with their oil, bell peppers, and serrano pepper.
- Sauté the vegetables until the peppers are tender. Add chicken drumsticks back to the skillet and serve immediately. Bon appétit!

9. Chicken Soup with Soba Noodles
(Ready in about 5 hours 15 minutes | Servings 6)

Hearty, rich and warm chicken soup for body and soul. What could be more comforting in cold weather?
Per serving: 370 Calories; 9.8g Fat; 15.5g Carbs; 52.5g Protein; 3.9g Sugars

Ingredients

3 pounds chicken back
5 cups vegetable broth, preferably homemade
1 yellow onion, peeled and chopped
2 parsnips, diced
3 carrots, diced
2 celery stalks, diced
2 bay leaves

Salt, to taste
1 teaspoon red pepper flakes, crushed
1/2 teaspoon freshly ground black pepper
2 cups dried soba noodles
1 handful fresh parsley, chopped
1/4 cup fresh coriander, coarsely chopped

Directions

- Preheat a sous vide water bath to 160 degrees F.
- Add the chicken, broth, onion, parsnip, carrots, celery and bay leaves to a large-sized cooking pouch.
- Now, submerge the cooking pouch in the water bath; let it simmer for 5 hours. Reserve the chicken back; remove meat from bones; cut the meat into bite-size pieces.
- Transfer the cooking liquid and vegetables to a stockpot. Bring this mixture to a boil. Add the salt, red pepper flakes, black pepper, and soba noodles to the stockpot.
- Reduce the temperature and cook approximately 9 minutes. Add the chicken meat back to the stockpot. Stir in the parsley and coriander.
- Cook for a further 2 to 3 minutes and ladle into soup bowls. Enjoy!

10. Hot Broiled Chicken Drumsticks
(Ready in about 3 hours 10 minutes | Servings 6)

These chicken drumsticks will change your perception of poultry. Juicy, appetizing and flavorsome, they are sure to please.
Per serving: 224 Calories; 12g Fat; 3.7g Carbs; 23.9g Protein; 2.2g Sugars

Ingredients

3 cups water
1/4 cup sea salt
1 tablespoon sugar
2 garlic cloves, pressed
1 tablespoon mixed peppercorns
3 sprigs rosemary

3 sprigs thyme
1 cinnamon stick
1 (1-inch) piece fresh ginger, grated
1/2 lime, zest and juice
6 chicken drumsticks
1/2 cup hot sauce

Directions

- In a large-sized mixing bowl, thoroughly combine the water, salt, sugar, garlic, spices, ginger, and lemon juice.
- Add the chicken drumsticks to the mixing bowl; place in your refrigerator and let it stand overnight.
- On an actual day, preheat a sous vide water bath to 160 degrees F.
- After that, rinse chicken drumsticks with a running water. Place the chicken drumsticks in cooking pouches and seal them tightly.
- Now, submerge the cooking pouches in the water bath; let it simmer for 3 hours. Remove the chicken drumsticks from the cooking pouches.
- Line the bottom of a broiler pan with a sheet of foil. Arrange chicken drumsticks on the broiler pan. Broil for 3 minutes; flip over and broil for another 3 minutes.
- Serve with hot sauce on the side. Bon appétit!

11. Arabic Chicken Masala
(Ready in about 2 hours | Servings 4)

This sous vide chicken tenderloin goes great with hot penne pasta. If you get lucky to save some leftovers, top it on a homemade crusty bread and serve for dinner.

Per serving: 565 Calories; 13.2g Fat; 31.5g Carbs; 75.2g Protein; 5.7g Sugars

Ingredients

1 pound chicken tenderloin, cut into pieces

1 tablespoon butter

1/2 cup leeks, sliced

2 garlic cloves, smashed

1 teaspoon curry powder

1/2 teaspoon cayenne pepper

1 teaspoon Arabic mix masala seasoning

1 tablespoon Tandori masala

2 teaspoons coriander powder

1/2 cup tomato sauce

2 ripe tomatoes, pureed

1 chicken cube stock seasoning

2 cups water

1 (16-ounce) box penne pasta

Directions

- Preheat a sous vide water bath to 150 degrees F. Rinse the chicken tenderloin and pat it dry.
- Melt the butter in a nonstick skillet that is preheated over a moderate flame. Now, brown the chicken pieces on all sides.
- Place the chicken in cooking pouches; add the remaining ingredients and seal tightly.
- Submerge the cooking pouches in the water bath; cook for 1 hour 30 minutes.
- When the chicken masala has 20 minutes left to cook, cook penne according to package directions.
- Drain penne pasta and divide among serving bowl. Pour chicken masala over penne and enjoy!

---

12. Old-Fashioned Chicken Stew
(Ready in about 1 hour 45 minutes | Servings 4)

An old-fashioned chicken stew is as delicious as it looks! It's fantastic spooned over hot pasta, basmati rice or millet.

Per serving: 395 Calories; 25.1g Fat; 12.5g Carbs; 30.3g Protein; 5.9g Sugars

Ingredients

1 tablespoon olive oil

6 chicken thighs

2 shallots, chopped

1 serrano pepper, deveined and chopped

2 medium-sized bell peppers, deveined and chopped

1 (1.5-inch) fresh ginger root, peeled and grated

1/4 cup port wine

1 parsnip, chopped

2 medium-sized carrots, chopped

2 ripe tomatoes, pureed

1 teaspoon garlic paste

2 bay leaves

1 teaspoon cayenne pepper

1 teaspoon adobo seasoning

2 cups water

1 tablespoon chicken bouillon granules

1/4 teaspoon ground black pepper

1/2 cup fresh chives, roughly chopped

Directions

- Heat a skillet over medium-high heat; add the olive oil. Sear the chicken thighs for 2 to 3 minutes per side; reserve.
- Add the shallots, peppers, and ginger, and sauté them in pan drippings until tender and fragrant. Add a splash of wine to deglaze the pan.
- Transfer the sautéed mixture to a large-sized cooking pouch; add reserved chicken thighs.
- Add the parsnip, carrots, tomatoes, garlic paste, bay leaves, cayenne pepper, adobo seasoning, water, chicken bouillon granules, and ground black pepper.
- Preheat a sous vide water bath to 165 degrees F. Submerge the cooking pouches in the water bath; cook for 1 hour 40 minutes.
- Ladle the stew into individual bowls; serve garnished with fresh chopped chives. Bon appétit!

13. Cheesy and Saucy Chicken Meatballs
(Ready in about 1 hour | Servings 5)

You can substitute 1/2 pound of lean ground pork or ground veal for the ground chicken. Swiss cheese will add some extra oomph to these meatballs.
Per serving: 488 Calories; 31.1g Fat; 19.1g Carbs; 35.1g Protein; 8.1g Sugars

Ingredients

1 ½ pounds ground chicken

3/4 cup cream cheese

1 cup tortilla crumbs

1 teaspoon dried parsley flakes

1/3 cup Romano cheese, grated

2 egg, well whisked

2 tablespoons scallions, finely minced

2 cloves garlic, finely minced

Salt and freshly ground black pepper, to taste

1/2 teaspoon cayenne pepper

1 teaspoon steak seasoning mix

10 small cubes of sharp Swiss cheese

2 tablespoons extra-virgin olive oil

2 ½ cups tomato puree

1 teaspoon jalapeno pepper, minced

Directions

- Preheat a sous vide water bath to 144 degrees F.
- In a mixing bowl, thoroughly combine the chicken, cream cheese, tortilla crumbs, dried parsley flakes, Romano cheese, eggs, scallions, garlic, salt, black pepper, cayenne pepper and steak seasoning mix.
- Shape the mixture into 10 equal balls. Add 1 cube of Swiss cheese to the center of each meatball, sealing meat tightly around cheese.
- Place the meatballs in cooking pouches; seal tightly. Submerge the cooking pouches in the water bath; cook for 50 minutes.
- Pat the meatballs dry and set them aside.
- Add the oil to a frying pan that is preheated over a moderate heat. Now, brown your meatballs on all sides, working in batches.
- When the meatballs are slightly crisp, remove them from the heat and place on a platter.
- Immediately add the tomato puree and minced jalapeno to the frying pan and bring it to a boil; reduce the heat and cook until the sauce has thickened slightly.
- Afterwards, ladle the sauce over the prepared meatballs and serve. Bon appétit!

14. Chicken Sausage with Mashed Potatoes
(Ready in about 1 hour | Servings 6)

With a sous vide chicken sausage, your family dinner becomes a breeze! In this recipe, you can experiment with seasonings and adjust them to suit your taste!
Per serving: 404 Calories; 11.5g Fat; 30.3g Carbs; 42.6g Protein; 4.2g Sugars

Ingredients

For the Sausage:

2 ½ pounds natural-casing raw chicken sausage

1/2 cup stock, preferably homemade

1/4 teaspoon ground black pepper

1 teaspoon sugar

1 tablespoon wine vinegar

2 tablespoons lard, softened

For the Mashed Potatoes:

1 ¼ pounds potatoes, peeled and quartered

1/2 cup whole milk

2 teaspoons butter

Salt and ground black pepper, to taste

1 teaspoon paprika

1 teaspoon parsley flakes

Directions

- Preheat a sous vide water bath to 150 degrees F. Place sausage, stock, black pepper, sugar, and wine vinegar in cooking pouches; seal tightly.
- Submerge the cooking pouches in the water bath; cook for 50 minutes. Pat sous vide sausage dry with kitchen towels.
- In a cast-iron skillet, melt the lard over a moderate heat. Now, brown sausages for 2 to 3 minutes on each side.
- In the meantime, add a lightly salted water to a pot; bring to a rapid boil. Now, boil the potatoes until fork tender, about 14 minutes; drain.
- Then, warm the milk and butter in a saucepan over low heat. Now, blend the milk/butter mixture into cooked potatoes using a potato masher.
- Add the salt, pepper, paprika, and parsley flakes. Serve with prepared chicken sausage. Bon appétit!

15. Classic Chicken Goulash with Mushrooms
(Ready in about 5 hours 5 minutes | Servings 6)

Use caramelized, sweated, or seared onions to enhance the flavor of your goulash. You can also play around with the spices to see what flavors you like best.

Per serving: 401 Calories; 17.1g Fat; 8.4g Carbs; 54.9g Protein; 4.2g Sugars

Ingredients

2 ½ pounds chicken drumettes, skin-on, bone-in

4 cups chicken stock

2 celery with leaves, peeled and diced

3 carrots, trimmed and sliced

1 large-sized onion, chopped

Sea salt, to taste

1/2 teaspoon ground black pepper

1/2 teaspoon hot paprika

2 tablespoons grapeseed oil

3 garlic cloves, chopped

2 cups brown mushrooms, sliced

1 tablespoon red curry paste

1 ½ teaspoons ground coriander

1/4 teaspoon dried thyme

2 bay leaves

2 tablespoons fresh parsley, chopped

1 tablespoon brown sugar

1 tablespoon oyster sauce

1/2 cup fresh chives, roughly chopped

Directions

- Preheat a sous vide water bath to 149 degrees F.
- Add the chicken drumettes, stock, celery, carrots, onion, salt, black pepper, and paprika to the cooking pouches; seal tightly.
- Submerge the cooking pouches in the water bath; cook for 4 hours.
- After that, remove the chicken from the cooking liquid and allow it to cool for 30 minutes. Now, chop the meat and discard the bones. Reserve the cooking liquid and vegetable solids.
- In a large pot, heat the oil over a moderate flame. Now, sauté the garlic until aromatic or about 1 minute; add mushrooms and cook an additional 3 minutes.
- Next, stir in the curry paste, coriander, thyme, bay leaves, fresh parsley, brown sugar, and oyster sauce. Continue to cook for a further 3 minutes.
- Then, add the reserved chicken along with cooking liquid and vegetable solids; cover with the lid and allow it to simmer for 25 minutes. Serve topped with fresh chopped chives. Bon appétit!

---

16. Chicken and Conecuh Sausage Jambalaya
(Ready in about 2 hours 50 minutes | Servings 4)

This sous vide Jambalaya is a great wintertime dish and it's really amazing, especially when served with a fresh or pickled salad. The chicken thighs and sausage are first cooked sous vide and then, added to the cooking pouch, ensuring all flavors are well blended.

Per serving: 611 Calories; 30.8g Fat; 53.4g Carbs; 29.1g Protein; 5.9g Sugars

Ingredients

2 tablespoons olive oil

1 pound chicken thighs, boneless and cubed

1/2 pound Conecuh sausage, cut bite-sized pieces

1 red bell pepper, seeded and sliced

1 green bell pepper, seeded and sliced

1 celery stalk, chopped

1 cup carrots, chopped

2 white onions, peeled and chopped

3 garlic cloves, minced

2 bay leaves

Sea salt and ground black pepper, to taste

1 teaspoon dried sage, crushed

1 tablespoon Creole seasoning

1/2 teaspoon dried basil

1 teaspoon paprika

1 cup brown rice

2 ripe tomatoes, chopped

3 cups broth, preferably homemade

Directions

- Preheat a sous vide water bath to 180 degrees F.
- Heat a skillet over medium-high heat; add the olive oil. Sear the chicken thighs along with Conecuh sausage approximately 6 minutes, turning once or twice; reserve.
- Add the peppers, celery, carrots, and onion; sauté the vegetables in pan drippings until tender and fragrant. Add a splash of broth to deglaze the pan.
- Transfer the sautéed mixture to a large-sized cooking pouch; add reserved chicken thighs and sausage. Add the remaining ingredients.
- Submerge the cooking pouches in the water bath; cook for 2 hours 40 minutes.
- Ladle your jambalaya into individual bowls; serve garnished with fresh chopped scallions, if desired. Bon appétit!

17. Restaurant-Style Chicken Paprikash
(Ready in about 1 hour 20 minutes | Servings 4)

In this recipe, you can experiment with different cooking times and increase or lower the temperature several degrees.
Per serving: 490 Calories; 35.6g Fat; 8.4g Carbs; 33.4g Protein; 2.2g Sugars

Ingredients

1 tablespoon butter, melted

1 ½ pounds chicken thighs, cut into pieces

2 shallots, chopped

2 garlic cloves, minced

1 red bell pepper, chopped

1 chili pepper, chopped

2 ½ cups broth, preferably homemade

Sea salt, to taste

1/4 teaspoon ground black pepper

2 tablespoons Hungarian paprika

1/2 cup sour cream

1/4 cup fresh cilantro, chopped

Directions

- Preheat a sous vide water bath to 170 degrees F.
- Heat the butter in a skillet over medium-high heat. Sear the chicken pieces for 3 to 4 minutes; add the shallots and garlic and cook for 2 minutes more.
- Add the chicken mixture to a large-sized cooking pouch. Now, add the peppers, broth, salt, pepper, and paprika to the cooking pouch and seal it tightly.
- Submerge the cooking pouches in the water bath; cook for 1 hour 10 minutes. Ladle into soup bowls and serve topped with sour cream and fresh cilantro.

---

18. Chicken Legs in Dijon-Tarragon Sauce
(Ready in about 2 hours 10 minutes | Servings 4)

Are you tired of cooking boring poultry recipes? Same old, same old? This recipe shows a good way to take inexpensive chicken legs and turn them into the most incredible chicken dish ever!
Per serving: 301 Calories; 19.6g Fat; 8.1g Carbs; 21.7g Protein; 0.9g Sugars

Ingredients

1 pound chicken drumsticks, boneless

1/2 teaspoon sea salt

1/4 teaspoon freshly ground black pepper

1/2 teaspoon cayenne pepper

1 tablespoon olive oil

2 tablespoons dry white wine

1 tablespoon Worcestershire sauce

1/2 cup heavy cream

1 tablespoon all-purpose flour

1 tablespoon Dijon mustard

1 tablespoon fresh tarragon

Directions

- Preheat a sous vide water bath to 145 degrees F.
- Now, sprinkle the chicken legs with salt, black pepper, and cayenne pepper.
- Add the seasoned chicken legs to a cooking pouch and seal tightly. Submerge the cooking pouches in the water bath; cook for 2 hours.
- Heat olive oil in a deep pan over a moderately high heat. Now, sear the chicken legs for 2 to 3 minutes per side.
- Deglaze the pan with white wine. Place the chicken legs on a platter. Add Worcestershire sauce, cream, and flour to the pan.
- Cook until the sauce has slightly thickened; stir in Dijon mustard and tarragon. Spoon the sauce over the prepared chicken legs and serve immediately. Bon appétit!

19. Brined Tequila-Garlic Chicken
(Ready in about 6 hours | Servings 4)

The process of making juicy chicken thighs is surprisingly simple by using sous vide cooking. In addition, the chicken has never tasted so good.
Per serving: 472 Calories; 23.9g Fat; 25.7g Carbs; 37.2g Protein; 23g Sugars

Ingredients

1 gallon warm water
2/3 cup sugar
1/2 cup kosher salt
1/2 cup soy sauce
1/4 cup olive oil
1 ½ pounds chicken tights

1 teaspoon garlic paste
Freshly ground black pepper, to taste
1 teaspoon cayenne pepper
1 teaspoon marjoram
1 tablespoon fish sauce
1 tablespoon tequila

Directions

- Combine the water, sugar, 1/2 cup of kosher salt, soy sauce and olive oil in a container.
- Place chicken tights in the brine, cover, and refrigerate for 4 hours. Spread the chicken thighs with garlic paste.
- Preheat a sous vide water bath to 145 degrees F.
- Season the chicken thighs with black pepper, cayenne pepper, and marjoram. Add chicken thighs to a cooking pouch.
- Submerge the cooking pouches in the water bath; cook for 2 hours. Remove the chicken from the cooking pouch.
- Sear the chicken along with fish sauce and tequila in the preheated nonstick skillet until well browned. Serve right away and enjoy!

20. Classic Creamy Chicken Salad with Walnuts
(Ready in about 3 hours 35 minutes | Servings 4)

Comforting and irresistible, this healthy salad is loaded with protein and vitamins. Chicken and fresh veggies are definitely a match made in heaven!
Per serving: 340 Calories; 23.8g Fat; 3.7g Carbs; 27.3g Protein; 1.1g Sugars

Ingredients

1 pound chicken breast halves
1/2 teaspoon freshly ground black pepper
1/2 teaspoon salt
1 celery stalk, diced
A bunch of scallions, thinly sliced
1 cup fresh arugula

2 tablespoons parsley, chopped
1 tablespoon fresh dill, chopped
1 tablespoon balsamic vinegar
1 teaspoon yellow mustard
1/2 cup mayonnaise
3 tablespoons walnuts, chopped

Directions

- Preheat a sous vide water bath to 150 degrees F.
- Rinse the chicken and pat dry. Season the chicken with pepper and salt. Put the chicken breast halves into cooking pouches and seal tightly.
- Submerge the cooking pouches in the water bath; cook for 3 hours.
- Next, allow the chicken to cool in the cold water for 30 minutes. Transfer the chicken to a cutting board. Cut chicken crosswise into thin slices.
- Toss the chicken slices with the remaining ingredients, except for walnuts. Serve garnished with chopped walnuts. Enjoy!

21. Crunchy Baked Chicken Fingers
(Ready in about 5 hours 15 minutes | Servings 4)

This recipes helps create classic chicken fingers that are incredibly tender inside and crunchy outside. Serve with some roasted carrots and potatoes.
Per serving: 501 Calories; 20.8g Fat; 54.6g Carbs; 23g Protein; 5.6g Sugars

Ingredients

1 ½ pounds chicken fillets
1 teaspoon shallot powder
1/2 teaspoon porcini powder
1/2 teaspoon cayenne pepper
Kosher salt and ground black pepper, to taste
2 teaspoons garlic paste

2 small-sized eggs, whisked
3/4 cup buttermilk
3/4 cup all-purpose flour
1/2 cup tortilla chips, crushed
1/2 cup Parmesan cheese, grated
2 tablespoons butter, melted

Directions

- Preheat a sous vide water bath to 149 degrees F.
- Season the chicken fillets with shallot powder, porcini powder, cayenne pepper, salt, and black pepper.
- Now, spread the chicken fillets with an even coat of garlic paste.
- Put the chicken into cooking pouches and seal tightly. Submerge the cooking pouches in the water bath; cook for 2 hours.
- Cut the chicken into 1/2-inch strips. In a large resealable plastic bag, mix the eggs and buttermilk; add chicken strips to the bag and shake to coat well; place in your refrigerator for 3 hours.
- Drain the chicken strips. In another bag, mix the flour, tortilla chips and Parmesan cheese; add chicken strips to the bag and shake to coat well.
- Now, preheat your oven to 450 degrees F. Line a baking sheet with a piece of foil. Arrange chicken fingers on the baking sheet.
- Drizzle melted butter over chicken fingers and bake approximately 7 minutes; flip them over and bake an additional 5 minutes. Serve immediately.

---

22. Chicken Legs with Wild Chanterelles
(Ready in about 3 hours 10 minutes | Servings 4)

Cooking with sous vide allows you to keep the chicken legs the doneness you want. If you prefer tender meat, cook it at 149 degrees F. If you prefer the meat that falls off the bone, preheat a sous vide water bath to 167 degrees F.
Per serving: 362 Calories; 22.2g Fat; 9.9g Carbs; 24.2g Protein; 3.1g Sugars

Ingredients

1 pound chicken legs, skinless boneless
Sea salt and ground black pepper, to taste
1/2 teaspoon cayenne pepper
1/2 teaspoon dried thyme
2 tablespoons butter, at room temperature
1 yellow onion, chopped
1 teaspoon garlic, smashed

1 ½ cups Chanterelle mushrooms, sliced
1 cup cream of mushroom soup
1/4 cup dark rum
1/2 cup double cream
1 teaspoon stone ground mustard
A pinch of grated nutmeg
1/2 teaspoon mixed peppercorns

Directions

- Preheat a sous vide water bath to 167 degrees F.
- Now, season chicken legs with salt, black pepper, cayenne pepper, and dried thyme.
- Place the chicken in cooking pouches and seal tightly. Submerge the cooking pouches in the water bath; cook for 3 hours.
- Pat the chicken dry and allow it to cool slightly.
- Now, preheat a deep pan over a moderately high heat. Add the chicken along with the onion, garlic, mushrooms, and mushroom soup; cook for 3 minutes or until the mushrooms are fragrant.
- Add the dark rum, double cream, ground mustard, grated nutmeg, and mixed peppercorns. Cook until the sauce has reduced to your desired consistency. Bon appétit!

23. Perfect Chicken Gumbo
(Ready in about 2 hours 50 minutes | Servings 6)

An old-fashioned chicken gumbo is as delicious as it looks. Serve over hot rice and enjoy!

Per serving: 383 Calories; 27.6g Fat; 12.1g Carbs; 21.2g Protein; 4.9g Sugars

Ingredients

1 ½ pounds chicken thighs, skinless, boneless, cut into chunks
1/2 teaspoon sea salt
1/4 teaspoon freshly ground pepper, or more to taste
1 tablespoon lard, melted
2 yellow onions, chopped
2 bell peppers, deseeded and chopped
1 jalapeno pepper, deseeded and chopped
2 carrots, chopped
2 parsnips, chopped
2 celery stalk, chopped

2 cloves garlic, minced
1 ½ teaspoon hot paprika
1 teaspoon dried rosemary
1/2 teaspoon dried thyme
1/2 teaspoon dried marjoram
1/2 teaspoon ground bay leaf
2 tablespoons all-purpose flour
1 teaspoon filé powder
1 large-sized can tomatoes, crushed
2 cups vegetable broth, preferably homemade

Directions

- Preheat a sous vide water bath to 149 degrees F.
- Season the chicken thighs with salt and black pepper. Add the chicken to the cooking pouches and seal tightly.
- Submerge the cooking pouches in the water bath; cook for 2 ½ hours.
- Remove the chicken from the cooking pouches and pat dry with kitchen towels. Melt the lard in a large stockpot over medium-high heat.
- Now, sear the chicken for 2 minutes; reserve. Add the onions, pepper, carrots, parsnip, and celery; cook in pan drippings until the vegetables are just tender.
- Add the remaining ingredients, including the reserved chicken, and bring to a boil. Now, reduce the heat to medium-low, cover and allow your gumbo to simmer for 13 minutes.
- Ladle into serving bowls and serve. Bon appétit!

---

24. Chicken Garden Medley
(Ready in about 2 hours 5 minutes | Servings 5)

Looking for a hearty and satisfying chicken recipe? A warm, flavorful medley might be one of the most perfect family meals. Serve with lots of crusty bread and fresh salad.

Per serving: 212 Calories; 7.9g Fat; 21.2g Carbs; 16.1g Protein; 10.7g Sugars

Ingredients

10 chicken wings
Sea salt and ground black pepper, to taste
2 tablespoons olive oil, divided
2 shallots, diced
2 garlic cloves, minced
12 ounces canned tomatoes, crushed
1 eggplant, peeled and diced

1 red bell pepper, diced
1 serrano pepper, diced
1 parsnip, diced
2 bay leaves
1 teaspoon dried sage
1/2 teaspoon dried basil
1 teaspoon dried thyme

Directions

- Preheat a sous vide water bath to 145 degrees F.
- Season chicken wings with sea salt and ground black pepper. Add the chicken to the cooking pouches and seal tightly.
- Submerge the cooking pouches in the water bath; cook for 1 ½ hours.
- Heat a Dutch oven over a moderate flame; add olive oil. Once hot, sear the chicken wings an all sides; reserve.
- Now, sauté the shallots and garlic until they are fragrant. Stir in tomatoes, eggplant, peppers, parsnip, bay leaves, sage, basil, and thyme; bring to a boil.
- Return the reserved chicken to your Dutch oven. Turn the heat to medium-low and continue to simmer an additional 30 minutes.
- Ladle into individual bowls and serve warm. Enjoy!

DUCK & TURKEY

25. Herb-Grilled Turkey Breast Cutlets
(Ready in about 3 hours 5 minutes | Servings 4)

From now onwards, you can grill superlean turkey breast and have the most tender and superbly flavored poultry ever!
Per serving: 271 Calories; 5.1g Fat; 1.6g Carbs; 51.6g Protein; 0.7g Sugars

Ingredients

1 ½ pounds turkey breast cutlets
Salt and ground black pepper, to taste
2 teaspoons fresh basil leaves, chopped
2 teaspoons fresh mint leaves, chopped

1 tablespoon extra-virgin olive oil
2 Roma tomatoes, thinly sliced
2 tablespoons fresh parsley leaves, roughly chopped

Directions

- Preheat a sous vide water bath to 145 degrees F.
- Season the turkey breast cutlets with salt and black pepper.
- Add the turkey breast cutlets to the cooking pouches and seal tightly. Submerge the cooking pouches in the water bath; cook for 3 hours.
- In the meantime, in a small-sized mixing bowl, combine the basil, mint, and olive oil. Pat turkey breast cutlets dry with kitchen towels and rub with herb/oil mixture on all sides.
- Prepare your grill for direct grilling on medium. Then, grill turkey breast cutlets about 4 minutes, flipping over once or twice.
- Serve turkey breast cutlets topped with tomato and fresh parsley. Enjoy!

---

26. The Best Thanksgiving Turkey Ever
(Ready in about 12 hours | Servings 12)

When it comes to the holiday season, a turkey roast simply must appear on the table. For the next holiday party, cook the bird sous vide and see the difference.
Per serving: 477 Calories; 38.1g Fat; 1.2g Carbs; 30.1g Protein; 1.1g Sugars

Ingredients

1 (13-pound) turkey, rinsed, patted dry
Coarse salt and ground black pepper, to taste
1 tablespoon dried thyme
1 tablespoon dried rosemary
1 tablespoon dried sage
1 ½ teaspoons garlic powder

1 teaspoon mustard seed
1 teaspoon paprika
1 tablespoon maple syrup
1 teaspoon fresh ginger, grated
A knob of butter, room temperature

Directions

- Preheat a sous vide water bath to 150 degrees F.
- Break down turkey into four pieces: two breasts and two legs. Now, remove the backbone.
- Then, thoroughly combine the salt, black pepper, thyme, rosemary, sage, garlic powder, mustard seeds, paprika, maple syrup, and fresh ginger.
- Spread the all of the pieces with this rub on both sides.
- Place the legs in cooking pouches and seal tightly. Submerge the cooking pouches in the water bath
- Place the turkey breasts in separate cooking pouches and place in your refrigerator.
- Cook the turkey legs for 7 hours.
- Reduce the water bath to 140 digress F. Add turkey breasts to cooking pouches and seal tightly. Submerge the cooking pouches in the water bath; cook for 4 to 5 hours; pat them dry.
- Melt the butter in a pan that is preheated over a moderately high heat. Now, sear the turkey until it looks golden brown.
- To serve, slice each piece into four or five portions and arrange on a platter. Enjoy!

27. Turkey Drumettes with Mango Salsa
(Ready in about 6 hours 15 minutes | Servings 4)

Prepare a mango salsa to dress up your turkey drumettes and bring Caribbean flavors into your kitchen during the winter season. Enjoy!
Per serving: 417 Calories; 19.9g Fat; 17.8g Carbs; 41.6g Protein; 13.6g Sugars

Ingredients

2 tablespoons butter, melted
1 pound turkey drumettes, skin-on, bone-in
Salt and pepper, to your liking

For the Mango Salsa:
1 mango, peeled and diced
1 cucumber, peeled and diced
1 garlic clove, minced

1 teaspoon chili pepper, minced
1/2 cup scallions, chopped
2 teaspoons fresh lime juice
1/4 cup fresh cilantro leaves, chopped
1/2 teaspoon sea salt
1/4 teaspoon ground black pepper
1/2 teaspoon red pepper flakes, crushed

Directions

- Melt 1 tablespoon of butter in a sauté pan and add the turkey drumettes, skin side down. Sear the turkey for 2 minutes per side.
- Preheat a sous vide water bath to 148 degrees F.
- Season the turkey with salt and black pepper to your liking; add them to cooking pouches and seal tightly.
- Submerge the cooking pouches in the water bath; cook for 6 hours.
- Adjust the broiling pan about 4 inches from the heat; now, broil the turkey, bone side to the heat, approximately 10 minutes, basting with the remaining tablespoon of melted butter.
- Meanwhile, make the mango salsa by mixing all of the above salsa ingredients. Serve broiled turkey drumettes with mango salsa on the side. Bon appétit!

28. Springtime Turkey Salad
(Ready in about 3 hours 35 minutes | Servings 4)

Spread this salad on a homemade crusty bread! Serve with a cold pasta! It will melt in your mouth.
Per serving: 289 Calories; 17.6g Fat; 3.9g Carbs; 27.2g Protein; 2.6g Sugars

Ingredients

1 pound turkey breast, boneless
Coarse salt and black pepper, to taste
1/2 cup green onions, chopped
1 bell pepper

1/2 cup radishes, sliced
1 teaspoon Dijon mustard
1/2 cup mayonnaise
1/2 tablespoon balsamic vinegar

Directions

- Preheat a sous vide water bath to 145 degrees F.
- Season the turkey breast with salt and black pepper.
- Add the turkey breast to the cooking pouches and seal tightly. Submerge the cooking pouches in the water bath; cook for 3 hours.
- Next, allow the turkey breast to cool in the cold water for 30 minutes. Transfer the turkey meat, to a food processor. Then, chop the meat using the pulse setting.
- Toss the chopped turkey with the remaining ingredients. Serve well chilled and enjoy!

29. Turkey and Mushroom Patties
(Ready in about 1 hour 5 minutes | Servings 4)

Have you ever cooked your turkey patties sous vide? Get ready for some insanely juicy, seriously delicious patties! To make your life easier, press the meat mixture into a ring mold.

Per serving: 295 Calories; 11.7g Fat; 23.8g Carbs; 25.5g Protein; 17.7g Sugars

Ingredients

1 pound turkey ground meat
1 egg, whisked
Salt and black pepper, to taste
1 teaspoon red pepper flakes, crushed
3/4 pound brown mushrooms, chopped
1 cup fine dry breadcrumb
1 onion, chopped

1 teaspoon garlic paste
1/2 teaspoon dried rosemary
1/2 teaspoon dried sage
1/2 teaspoon dried basil
1 teaspoon dry mustard powder
1 tablespoon olive oil

Directions

- Preheat a sous vide water bath to 145 degrees F.
- Thoroughly combine all of the above ingredients, except for olive oil, in a mixing dish.
- Shape the mixture into 1/2-inch thick patties.
- Add the patties to the cooking pouches and seal tightly. Submerge the cooking pouches in the water bath; cook for 1 hour.
- Next, heat the oil in a nonstick skillet and gently sear the patties about 1 minute per side or until golden brown
- Serve with dinner rolls and fresh salad, if desired. Bon appétit!

---

30. Norwegian-Style Duck Legs with Sandefjordsmor
(Ready in about 8 hours 15 minutes | Servings 4)

Sandefjordsmor is a traditional Norwegian butter sauce that goes wonderfully with sous vide poultry. It's perfect for those who love the unique flavor of duck.

Per serving: 295 Calories; 11.7g Fat; 23.8g Carbs; 25.5g Protein; 17.7g Sugars

Ingredients

1 pound duck legs
Sea salt and ground black pepper, to taste
1/2 teaspoon cayenne pepper
1 teaspoon mustard powder
1/2 teaspoon ground bay leaf
1 teaspoon fennel seeds
1/2 teaspoon shallot power
1/2 teaspoon garlic powder
1/2 teaspoon ginger powder
1 tablespoon olive oil

For Sandefjordsmor Sauce:
A juice of 1 fresh lemon
1/3 cup double cream
4 tablespoons cold butter
1/2 teaspoon sea salt
1/4 teaspoon freshly ground black pepper
1/4 cup loosely packed fresh parsley, chopped

Directions

- Preheat a sous vide water bath to 140 degrees F.
- Season duck legs with salt, black pepper, cayenne pepper, mustard powder, ground bay leaf, fennel seeds, shallot powder, garlic, and ginger powder.
- Place the duck legs in cooking pouches and seal tightly. Submerge the cooking pouches in the water bath; cook for 8 hours.
- Place olive oil in the skillet that is preheated over medium-high heat. Now, sear the duck legs 2 minutes per side and set them aside.
- Cook fresh lemon juice in a pan that is preheated over a moderate heat; allow it to simmer until the juice reduces to less than a tablespoon.
- Immediately whisk in double cream. Continue to whisk until the cream reduces; turn the heat to low.
- Gradually and slowly cut in the cold butter, whisking constantly; cook for about 7 minutes. Add salt, black pepper, and parsley; whisk to blend and remove from heat.
- Spoon the sauce over duck legs and serve.

31. Turkey Minestrone Soup
(Ready in about 6 hours 15 minutes | Servings 4)

A delicious and cozy, this soup might become your Thanksgiving favorite recipe. It's a good way to use up leftover meat, beans, and vegetables, too.
Per serving: 356 Calories; 17.6g Fat; 18.7g Carbs; 31.5g Protein; 2.6g Sugars

Ingredients

1 pound turkey thighs
1 tablespoon olive oil
2 shallots, chopped
1 red bell pepper, seeded and chopped
1 green bell pepper, seeded and chopped
1 celery with leaves, chopped
1 garlic clove, minced
4 ½ cups water

2 chicken bouillon cubes
Freshly ground black pepper, to taste
1/2 teaspoon dried thyme
1/2 pound broccoli, chopped into small florets
3 cups fresh Swiss chard
1/2 (15.5-ounce) can Great Northern beans
1/2 cup Parmesan cheese, freshly grated

Directions

- Preheat a sous vide water bath to 148 degrees F.
- Place the turkey thighs in cooking pouches and seal tightly. Submerge the cooking pouches in the water bath; cook for 6 hours.
- When the meat is cool enough to handle, strip the meat off the bones. Discard the bones and skin; cut the meat into 1 ½-inch chunks; reserve.
- In a large stockpot, heat the oil over a moderately high heat. Now, sauté the shallots until just tender and fragrant.
- Stir in the peppers, celery, and garlic; cook until they are tender.
- Add the water, bouillon cubes, black pepper, thyme, and broccoli; cook an additional 5 minutes.
- Bring to a boil; turn the heat to medium-low. Now, add the reserved turkey meat, Swiss chard, and beans; cook until the chard wilts.
- Serve topped with a freshly grated Parmesan cheese. Bon appétit!

32. Perfect Turkey Drumsticks with Gravy
(Ready in about 6 hours 20 minutes | Servings 8)

Discover how to make crispy and flavorful turkey drumsticks using a sous vide technique. In addition, you will have a recipe for the best holiday gravy you have ever tried.
Per serving: 463 Calories; 31.5g Fat; 8.5g Carbs; 34.3g Protein; 3g Sugars

Ingredients

4 pounds turkey drumsticks, skin-on, bone-in
1 teaspoon coarse salt
1/2 teaspoon freshly ground black pepper
1/2 teaspoon cayenne pepper
1/2 teaspoon dried rosemary
1 tablespoon butter

For the Gravy:
1 stick butter
2 yellow onions, peeled and chopped
1/4 cup all-purpose flour
Salt and pepper, to taste
5 cups turkey broth
1 tablespoon Cognac
1 tablespoon double cream

Directions

- Preheat a sous vide water bath to 148 degrees F.
- Season the turkey with the salt, black pepper, cayenne pepper, and rosemary; add the seasoned turkey drumsticks to cooking pouches and seal tightly.
- Submerge the cooking pouches in the water bath; cook for 6 hours.
- Now, melt 1 tablespoon of butter over a medium-high heat; sear the turkey drumsticks on all sides until the skin is brown and crisp.
- In a large pan, melt 1 stick of butter over medium-low heat; then, sauté the onions for 10 minutes or until they're lightly browned.
- Stir in the flour, salt, and pepper. Cook an additional 3 minutes. Now, pour in the hot turkey broth and Cognac; cook uncovered for 4 minutes or until the sauce has been thickened.
- Afterwards, whisk in the cream, stir and serve with the prepared turkey drumsticks.

33. Tortilla Chip-Crusted Turkey Fillets
(Ready in about 6 hours 20 minutes | Servings 4)

Sous vide turkey fillets go perfectly with tortilla chips, Romano cheese, and Dijon mustard in this appetizing restaurant-style dish.
Per serving: 425 Calories; 24.4g Fat; 6.8g Carbs; 42.4g Protein; 1.2g Sugars

Ingredients

1 ½ pounds turkey fillets
Salt and black pepper, to taste
1/2 teaspoon cayenne pepper
1 tablespoon Dijon mustard

1 tablespoon garlic paste
3/4 cup tortilla chips, crushed
1/2 cup Romano cheese, grated
2 tablespoons olive oil

Directions

- Preheat a sous vide water bath to 141 degrees F.
- Season the turkey fillets with salt, black pepper, and cayenne pepper. Now, add the seasoned turkey fillets to cooking pouches and seal tightly.
- Submerge the cooking pouches in the water bath; cook for 3 hours. Pat the turkey fillets dry; spread both sides of turkey fillets with Dijon mustard and garlic paste.
- In a shallow dish, thoroughly combine crushed tortilla chips and grated Romano cheese. Dredge the turkey fillets in this tortilla chips mixture.
- Heat the olive oil in a pan over a moderate heat. Now, cook turkey fillets for 6 minutes per side. Serve warm.

34. Homemade Duck Sausage
(Ready in about 7 hours 15 minutes | Servings 6)

Is there anything better to serve for dinner than a homemade poultry sausage? You can use a mixed pork meat like a pork shoulder and pork belly for these sausages.
Per serving: 425 Calories; 24.4g Fat; 6.8g Carbs; 42.4g Protein; 1.2g Sugars

Ingredients

1/2 teaspoon caraway seeds
1/2 teaspoon mustard seeds
1 teaspoon black pepper
1/2 teaspoon whole allspice berries
1 tablespoon rubbed sage
1 teaspoon ground bay leaf
4 teaspoons salt
2 teaspoon granulated garlic

1 pound pork, ground
1 pound duck breast, ground
7 ounces duck liver, ground
1/3 cup white wine
Natural sheep casings, for stuffing
1 tablespoon lard, room temperature
6 (6-inch) sandwich rolls

Directions

- Thoroughly combine all seasonings with ground meat and wine.
- Once the mixture is fully mixed, run the mixture through the grinder. Place in your refrigerator for 4 hours and allow it to cool completely.
- Now, stuff sausage mixture into casings.
- Preheat a sous vide water bath to 140 degrees F.
- Now, add the sausages to cooking pouches and seal tightly. Submerge the cooking pouches in the water bath; cook for 3 hours.
- Melt the lard in a skillet over a moderately high flame. Sear the sausage on all sides.
- Serve warm sausages with sandwich rolls and fresh salad, if desired. Bon appétit!

35. Oriental Duck Salad
(Ready in about 2 hours 5 minutes | Servings 4)

If you love to eat duck breasts but have always wished they were juicy and stringy at the same time, a sous vide duck might be right for you!
Per serving: 224 Calories; 7.3g Fat; 15.6g Carbs; 24.2g Protein; 12.2g Sugars

Ingredients

1 pound duck breasts, skinless and boneless

Maldon salt flakes, to taste

1/4 teaspoon freshly ground black pepper

2 cups rocket lettuce

1 red bell pepper, thinly sliced

1 carrot, shredded

2 tomatoes, diced

1/2 cup spring onions

For the Dressing:

1 ½ tablespoons extra-virgin olive oil

1 tablespoon apple cider vinegar

1 tablespoon fresh lime juice

1 teaspoon minced garlic

1/2 teaspoon sumac

1/2 teaspoon Maras pepper, crushed

2 tablespoons honey

Directions

- Preheat a sous vide water bath to 135 degrees F.
- Season the duck breasts with salt flakes and ground black pepper.
- Now, add the duck breast to cooking pouches and seal tightly. Submerge the cooking pouches in the water bath; cook for 2 hours.
- Then, slice the duck into strips and transfer to a salad bowl. Add rocket lettuce, bell pepper, carrot, tomatoes, and spring onions; toss to combine.
- In a small mixing bowl, thoroughly combine all of the dressing ingredients. Dress your salad and serve.

---

36. Turkey Breasts with Zingy Carrot Sauce
(Ready in about 5 hours 10 minutes | Servings 4)

Moist and flavorful sous vide turkey breasts and sweet carrot sauce work together to create a splendidly tasty family meal.
Per serving: 404 Calories; 19.1g Fat; 18.1g Carbs; 39.1g Protein; 11.2g Sugars

Ingredients

1 ½ pounds turkey breast, cut into pieces

Salt and pepper, to taste

1 teaspoon dried thyme

1 teaspoon juniper berries

2 tablespoons olive oil

1 shallot, chopped

1 pound carrots, finely sliced

1/4 cup mixed berry marmalade

1/4 cup broth, preferably homemade

1 tablespoon fresh orange juice

2 heaping tablespoons watercress

Directions

- Preheat a sous vide water bath to 140 degrees F.
- Season the turkey breasts with salt, pepper, and thyme.
- Now, add the seasoned turkey breast and juniper berries to cooking pouches and seal tightly. Submerge the cooking pouches in the water bath; cook for 5 hours.
- Heat a saucepan over a moderately high heat; add 1 tablespoon of olive oil. Once hot, sear the turkey breasts for 3 minutes on each side; reserve.
- Heat the remaining tablespoon of olive oil in a saucepan over a moderate heat. Sauté the shallot and carrots until tender.
- Stir in the marmalade, broth and orange juice; bring to a boil. Turn the heat to medium-low; allow it to simmer approximately 3 minutes.
- To serve, spoon the sauce over the turkey and add watercress on the top. Bon appétit!

37. Roasted Turkey Legs with Cauliflower
(Ready in about 10 hours 25 minutes | Servings 4)

Turkey legs are affordable and tasty pieces of turkey. Cooking them in the preheated water oven "locks" in the flavors and nutrients, making it a great Sunday dish.

Per serving: 365 Calories; 23.1g Fat; 3.6g Carbs; 34.7g Protein; 1.3g Sugars

Ingredients

1 ½ pounds turkey legs

1 teaspoon sea salt

1/2 teaspoon ground black pepper, to taste

1/2 teaspoon cayenne pepper

4 tablespoons butter

1 head cauliflower, cut into florets

1 teaspoon dried thyme

Directions

- Preheat a sous vide water bath to 165 degrees F.
- Season the turkey legs with salt, black pepper, and cayenne pepper; add the seasoned turkey legs to cooking pouches and seal tightly.
- Submerge the cooking pouches in the water bath; cook for 10 hours; pat the turkey legs dry and spread them with softened butter.
- Transfer buttered turkey legs to a lightly greased roasting pan. Scatter the cauliflower florets around them; sprinkle dried thyme over the cauliflower florets.
- Now, preheat your oven to 345 degrees F; bake for 20 minutes or until the skin is crisp and the cauliflower florets are fork tender. Bon appétit!

38. Turkey Thighs with Port Sauce
(Ready in about 6 hours 10 minutes | Servings 4)

Turkey thighs are flavored with wine and herb sauce. This is a delicious recipe you'll be asked to cook time and time again.

Per serving: 374 Calories; 23.1g Fat; 0.7g Carbs; 38.4g Protein; 0.3g Sugars

Ingredients

4 turkey thighs

1/2 teaspoon celery salt

Ground black pepper, to taste

2 tablespoons butter

1/2 cup Port wine

1 sprig thyme, chopped

1 sprig rosemary, chopped

1/2 teaspoon caraway seeds

1 teaspoon mustard seeds

Directions

- Preheat a sous vide water bath to 141 degrees F.
- Season the thighs with celery salt and black pepper; add the seasoned turkey thighs to cooking pouches and seal tightly.
- Submerge the cooking pouches in the water bath; cook for 6 hours.
- Melt the butter in a pan over medium-high heat. Sear the turkey thighs for 1 to 2 minutes.
- Add the remaining ingredients, and cook, partially covered, basting turkey with cooking liquids periodically.
- Reserve the turkey thighs; continue to cook the liquid until it has thickened to your desired doneness. Serve the turkey with Port sauce and enjoy!

39. Turkey Cutlets with Mashed Potatoes
(Ready in about 6 hours 20 minutes | Servings 4)

Wow a festive dinner table with this amazing sous vide turkey recipe! With sous vide turkey that is done ahead of time, holiday cooking becomes a breeze!

Per serving: 528 Calories; 19.4g Fat; 43.7g Carbs; 42.9g Protein; 6.8g Sugars

Ingredients

1 ½ pounds turkey cutlets
Sea salt and ground black pepper, to your liking
1 teaspoon poultry seasoning
Zest of 1/2 lemon
1 tablespoon peanut oil

For the Mashed Potatoes:
1 pound baking potatoes, peeled and quartered
1/2 cup whole milk
1 tablespoon butter
1 teaspoon fine sea salt
1/4 teaspoon ground black pepper, or more to taste
1 heaping tablespoon fresh parsley, roughly chopped

Directions

- Preheat a sous vide water bath to 140 degrees F.
- Season the turkey cutlets with salt, black pepper, and poultry seasoning; add the seasoned turkey cutlets and lemon zest to cooking pouches and seal tightly.
- Submerge the cooking pouches in the water bath; cook for 6 hours.
- Warm the peanut oil in a nonstick skillet over medium-high heat. Sear the turkey cutlets approximately 2 minutes per side.
- Next, add a lightly salted water to a pot; bring to a rapid boil. Now, boil the potatoes until fork tender, about 15 minutes; drain.
- Then, warm the milk and butter in a saucepan over low heat; blend warm butter mixture into cooked potatoes; blend with a potato masher until smooth.
- Season with salt and black pepper; taste, adjust the seasonings, and serve immediately with prepared turkey cutlets. Garnish with fresh parsley. Bon appétit!

40. Sophisticated Pickle-Brined Duck
(Ready in about 3 hours 10 minutes | Servings 6)

Brining overnight and cooking duck sous vide keep it moist and flavorful. Extremely juicy and tender, these are not entry-level duck breasts.

Per serving: 253 Calories; 9.1g Fat; 11.3g Carbs; 30.6g Protein; 9.4g Sugars

Ingredients

2 pounds duck breasts
5 cups pickle juice
7 cups water
1/2 cup brown sugar
1 cup sea salt

1/2 teaspoon cayenne pepper
1/4 teaspoon ground black pepper
2 bay leaves
1 tablespoon olive oil

Directions

- Place duck breasts in a large bowl. Add pickle juice, water, sugar, salt, cayenne pepper, black pepper, and bay leaves. Place in the refrigerator overnight.
- Remove duck breasts from the brine and rinse them; pat dry with kitchen towels.
- Preheat a sous vide water bath to 131 degrees F; add the seasoned turkey cutlets to cooking pouches and seal tightly.
- Submerge the cooking pouches in the water bath; cook for 3 hours.
- After that, heat olive oil in a frying pan that is preheated over medium-high flame. Sear the duck breasts on all sides until the skin is nice and crisp.
- Serve over hot cooked jasmine rice if desired. Bon appétit!

41. Delicious Herby and Garlicky Duck
(Ready in about 8 hours 10 minutes | Servings 6)

Annato oil is appreciated for its unique flavor and divine orange color and it works well in this recipe. However, if you don't have annato oil, feel free to use olive oil, peanut oil or grapeseed oil.

Per serving: 310 Calories; 19.2g Fat; 1.5g Carbs; 31g Protein; 0.4g Sugars

Ingredients

2 duck drumsticks
2 duck wings
Sea salt and ground black pepper, to taste
1/2 teaspoon paprika
1 teaspoon mustard powder
1 teaspoon granulated garlic
1/2 teaspoon onion powder

1 tablespoon annatto oil
2 cloves garlic, crushed
1 tablespoon dried rosemary
1 tablespoon dried sage
1 teaspoon dried basil
1/2 teaspoon dried oregano

Directions

- Preheat a sous vide water bath to 140 degrees F.
- Season the duck with salt, pepper, paprika, mustard powder, granulated garlic, and onion powder.
- Now, add the seasoned duck drumsticks to a large cooking pouch and seal tightly. Add the duck wings to another cooking pouch and seal tightly.
- Submerge the cooking pouches in the water bath; cook for 4 hours.
- Remove the duck wings form the water bath. Increase the temperature to 176 degrees F and continue to cook drumsticks an additional 4 hours.
- Heat annatto oil in a pan that is preheated over a moderately high heat. Sauté freshly crushed garlic along with the remaining herbs until they are aromatic.
- Add duck drumsticks and wings and sear briefly, coating them with garlic/herb mixture on all sides. Serve immediately. Enjoy!

---

42. Luxurious Foie Gras
(Ready in about 40 minutes | Servings 2)

For this recipe, make sure to find grade-A duck foie gras, it's worth the effort. A pinch of salt and freshly ground black pepper is all you need to make a pure perfection.

Per serving: 215 Calories; 12.1g Fat; 4.1g Carbs; 21.2g Protein; 0g Sugars

Ingredients

1 (1/2-pound) piece foie gras, cleaned and deveined, at room temperature
Sea salt and freshly ground black pepper, to taste

1 tablespoon grapeseed oil
2 heaping tablespoon cilantro leaves

Directions

- Preheat a sous vide water bath to 134 degrees F.
- Season duck foie gras with salt and pepper. Now, cut it into thick rounds.
- Now, add the seasoned duck foie gras to a large cooking pouch and seal tightly. Submerge the cooking pouches in the water bath; cook for 35 minutes.
- Heat the oil in a heavy skillet over medium-high heat. Once hot, sear the foie gras about 1 minute per side.
- Serve topped with fresh cilantro leaves. Bon appétit!

43. Duck Stew with White Wine
(Ready in about 3 hours 15 minutes | Servings 4)

Cooking a duck sous vide reduces the risk of the meat drying out in the end. This recipe is the holy grail for anyone in search of holiday stew recipe.

Per serving: 420 Calories; 21.1g Fat; 22.1g Carbs; 35.8g Protein; 12.8g Sugars

Ingredients

1 tablespoon olive oil

4 duck legs

2 sweet onions, chopped

2 bell peppers, seeded and chopped

2 carrots, chopped

2 parsnips, chopped

2 ripe vine tomatoes, chopped

1 teaspoon fresh garlic, crushed

2 bay leaves

4 juniper berries

1 tablespoon dried sage

1 teaspoon dried basil

1/2 teaspoon ground black pepper

1/2 tablespoon cayenne pepper

1/3 teaspoon hot sauce

1 cup dry white wine

2 cups broth

Salt, to taste

Directions

- Heat olive oil in a pot that is preheated over a moderately high heat. Now, sear the duck legs for 3 to 4 minute on each side; reserve.
- Then, cook sweet onions in pan drippings until they are aromatic. Add the peppers, carrots, and parsnip; continue to cook until they're tender.
- Add the remaining ingredients; reduce the heat to medium-low, cover with the lid, and continue to simmer an additional 10 minutes.
- Preheat a sous vide water bath to 140 degrees F.
- Now, add the stewed vegetables along with the cooking liquid and duck drumsticks to cooking pouches; seal tightly.
- Submerge the cooking pouches in the water bath; cook for 3 hours. Serve warm and enjoy!

44. Cajun Turkey Drumsticks
(Ready in about 3 hours 40 minutes | Servings 4)

The key ingredients in this turkey recipe are Cajun seasoning mix and peanut oil. Keep in mind that you can make your own Cajun seasoning mix with common spices from your pantry – simply combine the garlic powder, onion powder, paprika, cayenne pepper, thyme, and oregano.

Per serving: 383 Calories; 18.1g Fat; 1.3g Carbs; 49.7g Protein; 0.2g Sugars

Ingredients

2 turkey breasts, skin-on, boneless

1 teaspoon sea salt

1/4 teaspoon ground black pepper, or more to taste

1 tablespoon Ragin' Cajun seasoning mix

2 teaspoons peanut oil

Directions

- Preheat a sous vide water bath to 149 degrees F.
- Season the turkey breast with salt, pepper, and Cajun seasoning mix.
- Now, add the seasoned turkey to a large cooking pouch and seal tightly. Submerge the cooking pouches in the water bath; cook for 3 hours 30 minutes.
- Remove the turkey breast from the cooking pouch, reserving the cooking liquid for a gravy.
- Heat the peanut oil in a pan over high heat. Sear the turkey breasts, skin-side down, until light golden brown, for 4 to 5 minutes.
- Flip the breasts over and cook an additional 3 minutes. Serve immediately.

45. Grilled Turkey Sausage with Fried Sauerkraut
(Ready in about 2 hours 20 minutes | Servings 4)

Grilled turkey sausage goes wonderfully with an aromatic fried sauerkraut. With sous vide, you're guaranteed tender, juicy and flavorful sausages every time.

Per serving: 354 Calories; 18.7g Fat; 19.9g Carbs; 21.2g Protein; 1.6g Sugars

Ingredients

1 pound raw turkey sausage
1 can beer
1/2 cup broth, preferably homemade
2 tablespoons grapeseed oil
2 garlic cloves, smashed

2 ½ cups sauerkraut, drained
1/2 teaspoon black peppercorns
1 teaspoon cayenne pepper
1/4 teaspoon cumin powder
2 bay leaves

Directions

- Preheat a sous vide water bath to 150 degrees F.
- Now, add raw turkey sausage to a large cooking pouch; pour in the beer and broth and seal tightly.
- Submerge the cooking pouches in the water bath; cook for 2 hours.
- Meanwhile, heat the grapeseed oil in a saucepan over a moderate heat. Sauté the garlic until fragrant.
- Add the sauerkraut and cook for a further 5 minutes.
- Now, add black peppercorns, cayenne pepper, cumin powder, and bay leaves. Cover with the lid and continue to simmer an additional 7 to 10 minutes.
- Take sous vide sausages out of cooking pouches; pat them dry with paper towels.
- Place the sausages on the grill. Grill for 2 to 3 minutes per side or until they have char marks. Serve the grilled sausages with a sauerkraut on the side. Bon appétit!

---

46. Honey Teriyaki Turkey Breasts
(Ready in about 2 hours 40 minutes | Servings 4)

The idea behind this recipe is to allow some common ingredients to really shine. With this cooking time, the turkey breasts are moist and tender.

Per serving: 414 Calories; 19.1g Fat; 17.2g Carbs; 39g Protein; 12.7g Sugars

Ingredients

1 ½ pounds turkey breasts
1/2 teaspoon coarse salt
1/2 teaspoon ground black pepper
1/2 teaspoon cayenne pepper
1 tablespoon peanut oil
2 cloves garlic, minced

1 tablespoon fresh ginger, grated
1/4 cup soy sauce
2 tablespoons rice wine vinegar
2 tablespoons sake
2 tablespoons honey
1 tablespoon cornstarch

Directions

- Preheat a sous vide water bath to 145 degrees F. Season turkey breasts with salt, black pepper, and cayenne pepper.
- Now, add raw turkey breasts to cooking pouches and seal tightly.
- Submerge the cooking pouches in the water bath; cook for 2 hours 30 minutes. Pat the turkey dry and set it aside.
- Heat peanut oil in a skillet over medium-high heat. Once hot, add the garlic and grated ginger; sauté until they are fragrant.
- Add the remaining ingredients and whisk well to combine; add the sous vide turkey breasts. Cook over a moderate heat until the sauce has reduced slightly and turkey is cooked through.
- Serve over hot cooked rice. Enjoy!

47. Duck Cutlets in Cognac-Cream Sauce
(Ready in about 1 hour 15 minutes | Servings 4)

Perfect for festive dinner, this recipe is certain to wow your guests. Serve with lots of fresh salad.
Per serving: 399 Calories; 28.8g Fat; 2.3g Carbs; 21.4g Protein; 2.2g Sugars

Ingredients

1 pound duck cutlets
Sea salt and freshly ground black pepper, to taste
1/4 teaspoon ground bay leaf
1/2 teaspoon fresh rosemary

1 teaspoon fresh thyme
1 cup double cream
1/3 cup cognac
1 tablespoon fresh cilantro

Directions

- Preheat a sous vide water bath to 135 degrees F.
- Season the duck breasts with salt, ground black pepper, ground bay leaf, rosemary, and thyme.
- Now, add the duck breast to cooking pouches and seal tightly. Submerge the cooking pouches in the water bath; cook for 1 hour.
- Heat a nonstick skillet over a moderately high heat. Add the cream and cognac; add sous vide duck breasts.
- Then, cook approximately 13 minutes or until the sauce has reduced slightly. Serve warm topped with fresh cilantro. Bon appétit!

48. Pasta with Spicy Turkey Meatballs
(Ready in about 5 hours 10 minutes | Servings 6)

Here's an all-star meatballs recipe with slowly cooked ground meat, fresh herbs, two types of peppers, and hot pasta. A perfect way to amaze your family and friends for holidays!
Per serving: 424 Calories; 18g Fat; 30.4g Carbs; 35.6g Protein; 3.3g Sugars

Ingredients

1 ½ pounds turkey, ground
1/2 pounds pork, ground
1/4 cup tomato paste
1 cup leeks, chopped
1 jalapeno pepper, seeded and finely chopped
1 tablespoon fresh bell pepper, seeded and finely chopped
2 tablespoons fresh coriander, chopped

1 ½ tablespoons soy sauce
2 cloves garlic, minced
Salt and freshly ground black pepper, to your liking
1 teaspoon cayenne pepper
1 tablespoon lard
18 ounces pasta of choice

Directions

- In a mixing bowl, combine the ground turkey, pork, tomato paste, leeks, peppers, coriander, soy sauce, garlic, salt, black pepper, and cayenne pepper. Mix until everything is well incorporated.
- Shape the mixture into balls. Next, place them in your freezer for 3 ½ hours.
- Preheat a sous vide water bath to 145 degrees F.
- Now, add the frozen meatballs to cooking pouches and seal tightly. Submerge the cooking pouches in the water bath; cook for 1 hour 30 minutes.
- Melt the lard in a pan over medium-high heat. Sear the meatballs on all sides until they are browned and crisp.
- Cook the pasta according to package directions. Serve the meatballs over the cooked pasta and enjoy!

PORK

49. Pork Chops in Creamy Vidalia Sauce
(Ready in about 6 hours 50 minutes | Servings 4)

Blade chops are cut from tougher parts of the pig. That's where sous vide comes in. Serve over hot cooked rice or your favorite pasta.
Per serving: 386 Calories; 21.5g Fat; 7.6g Carbs; 38.8g Protein; 2.9g Sugars

Ingredients

1 ½ pounds pork blade chops
1/2 teaspoon kosher salt
1/2 teaspoon paprika
1/4 teaspoon ground black pepper
2 tablespoons olive oil

1/2 pound Vidalia onions, sliced into rings
1/2 cup beef stock
1 teaspoon mustard powder
6 ounces sour cream

Directions

- Preheat a sous vide water bath to 141 degrees F.
- Season blade chops with salt, paprika, and pepper.
- Now, add the blade chops to cooking pouches and seal tightly. Submerge the cooking pouches in the water bath; cook for 6 hours 30 minutes.
- Pat the chops dry with paper towels.
- Then, heat the oil in a saucepan over a moderately high heat. Sauté Vidalia onions until they are tender and caramelized, about 6 to 7 minutes.
- Add the beef stock and mustard powder; add the reserved pork. Reduce the heat and continue to simmer an additional 5 minutes.
- Stir in the sour cream and continue to cook for a further 4 minutes. Serve on individual plates and enjoy!

---

50. Easy and Saucy Pork Sirloin Chops
(Ready in about 5 hours 15 minutes | Servings 4)

Why choose either moist but with no crust or crispy but dry pork chops? As a matter of fact, you can have it all!
Per serving: 386 Calories; 21.5g Fat; 7.6g Carbs; 38.8g Protein; 2.9g Sugars

Ingredients

1 ½ pounds pork sirloin chops
1/2 teaspoon salt
1/4 teaspoon freshly ground black pepper
1/2 teaspoon cayenne pepper
1/2 teaspoon dried oregano
1 teaspoon dried basil

1 teaspoon smashed garlic
1/2 cup broth, preferably homemade
2 tablespoons olive oil
1 cup leeks, chopped
2 bell pepper, seeded and chopped

Directions

- Preheat a sous vide water bath to 140 degrees F.
- Now, season pork sirloin chops with salt, black pepper, cayenne pepper, oregano, basil, and garlic.
- After that, add the pork sirloin chops and broth to cooking pouches and seal tightly. Submerge the cooking pouches in the water bath; cook for 8 hours.
- Pat the pork chops dry with paper towels, reserving the cooking liquid.
- Heat the oil in a skillet that is preheated over a moderately high heat. Sear the pork sirloin chops for 3 minutes per side; reserve.
- Then, sauté the leeks and peppers in pan drippings until they are tender; add a splash of reserved cooking liquid.
- Now, cook until the sauce has thickened slightly; add the reserved pork chops. Serve immediately. Bon appétit!

51. Traditional Side Pork
(Ready in about 12 hours 15 minutes | Servings 4)

Are you ready for the best side pork you have ever tried? In addition to the tasty flavor, this dish has a great texture and traditional charm.
Per serving: 539 Calories; 25.3g Fat; 13.7g Carbs; 60g Protein; 0.9g Sugars

Ingredients

2 pounds side pork

Salt and pepper, to taste

1 teaspoon Hungarian paprika

1 teaspoon shallot powder

1/2 teaspoon garlic powder

1/2 teaspoon mustard powder

1/2 cup all-purpose flour

Directions

- Preheat a sous vide water bath to 176 degrees F. Season the pork with salt and pepper.
- Now, add the seasoned side pork to a large-sized cooking pouch and seal tightly. Submerge the cooking pouch in the water bath; cook for 12 hours.
- Then, preheat your oven to 395 degrees F. Spritz a baking pan with a nonstick cooking spray.
- Spread side pork with Hungarian paprika, shallot powder, garlic powder, mustard powder and flour on both sides. Place it on the prepared baking pan.
- Roast the side pork for 10 to 15 minutes, turning halfway through cooking time. Bon appétit!

52. Oven Roasted Crispy Pork Belly
(Ready in about 13 hours 35 minutes | Servings 8)

With a right technique, a pork belly is ridiculously simple to prepare. This pork belly is deliciously tender and amazingly flavorful.
Per serving: 587 Calories; 60g Fat; 0g Carbs; 10.5g Protein; 0g Sugars

Ingredients

2 pounds pork belly

1 teaspoon salt

1/2 teaspoon ground black pepper

1/2 cup teaspoon hot paprika

1 teaspoon dried basil

1/2 teaspoon garlic powder

1/2 teaspoon mustard powder

1/2 teaspoon dried thyme

1 teaspoon dried rosemary

1 teaspoon dried parsley flakes

Directions

- Preheat a sous vide water bath to 176 degrees F.
- Then, season pork belly with all aromatics.
- Now, add the seasoned pork belly to a large-sized cooking pouch and seal tightly. Submerge the cooking pouch in the water bath; cook for 12 hours.
- Preheat your oven to 310 degrees F.
- Roast pork belly for 30 minutes, fat side up. Reduce heat to 280 degrees F and roast for an hour or until tender.
- Taste, adjust the seasoning and serve warm. Bon appétit!

53. Easy Country-Style Ribs
(Ready in about 20 hours 5 minutes | Servings 4)

When it comes to the country style ribs, tenderness is the key. Sous vide the ribs for 18 to 36 hours and then, broil or grill them briefly. Enjoy!
Per serving: 378 Calories; 19.5g Fat; 0g Carbs; 47.1g Protein; 0g Sugars

Ingredients

Salt and ground black pepper, to taste
1 tablespoon cayenne pepper
1 teaspoon chipotle powder
1 teaspoon garlic powder
1/2 teaspoon shallot powder

1 teaspoon dried marjoram
1 teaspoon dried rosemary
2 pounds country-style ribs
2 tablespoon grapeseed oil

Directions

- Preheat a sous vide water bath to 145 degrees F.
- Make the rub by mixing all of the above seasonings. Massage the rub all over the country-style ribs.
- Now, add the seasoned country style ribs to a large-sized cooking pouch and seal tightly. Submerge the cooking pouch in the water bath; cook for 20 hours.
- To broil the country style ribs, arrange them on a baking sheet. Drizzle the oil over the ribs.
- Place it under the broiler approximately 3 minutes. Bon appétit!

---

54. Grandma's Aromatic Pork Shoulder
(Ready in about 18 hours 10 minutes | Servings 6)

Have you ever had a pork shoulder in an old-fashioned way? It's time to try some grandma's recipes! Looks like the perfect family meal!
Per serving: 459 Calories; 31.3g Fat; 3.6g Carbs; 38.4g Protein; 1.3g Sugars

Ingredients

2 pounds pork shoulder
1/2 teaspoon cayenne pepper
Kosher salt, to taste
1/4 teaspoon ground black pepper, or more to taste
2 tablespoons olive oil
1 cup leeks, sliced

2 bell peppers, thinly sliced
1/3 cup dry red wine
1 teaspoon dried rosemary
1/2 teaspoon dried marjoram
1 teaspoon mustard seeds
1 teaspoon garlic, granulated

Directions

- Preheat a sous vide water bath to 165 degrees F.
- Season the pork shoulder generously with cayenne pepper, salt, and black pepper.
- Now, add the seasoned pork to a large-sized cooking pouch and seal tightly. Submerge the cooking pouch in the water bath; cook for 18 hours.
- Heat 1 tablespoon of olive oil in a frying pan over a moderately high heat; now, sear the sous vide pork shoulder on both sides until it is browned; reserve.
- Heat another tablespoon of olive oil and cook the leeks and peppers until tender and fragrant; add wine to deglaze the pan and continue to cook until it is evaporated.
- Add the remaining aromatics and cook an additional minute, stirring frequently.
- Add the pork shoulder back to the pan; stir and remove from heat. Serve immediately. Enjoy!

55. Pork Chili Verde
(Ready in about 14 hours 15 minutes | Servings 6)

This recipe is perfect but feel free to get creative with the flavors and add your favorite spices and vegetables.
Per serving: 314 Calories; 10.9g Fat; 13.9g Carbs; 39.3g Protein; 5.6g Sugars

Ingredients

1 tablespoon olive oil
2 ½ pounds blade roast, cubed
Sea salt and ground black pepper, to taste
1/2 teaspoon red pepper flakes
1/2 cup leeks, chopped
4 Poblano chilies, seeded and chopped

1 pound fresh tomatillos, husks removed
1 bunch fresh cilantro leaf, chopped

2 yellow bell peppers, seeded and chopped
4 garlic cloves, thinly sliced
1 tablespoon brown sugar
1 teaspoon dried Mexican oregano
3 cups broth

Directions

- Preheat a sous vide water bath to 176 degrees F.
- Add the oil to a nonstick skillet that is preheated over medium-high flame. Now, sear the pork until golden brown. Season with salt, black pepper, and red pepper flakes; reserve.
- Now, cook the leeks in pan drippings along with peppers and garlic; sauté approximately 8 minutes. Add brown sugar and Mexican oregano; cook an additional minute.
- Add the pork and broth to a large-sized cooking pouch and seal tightly. Submerge the cooking pouch in the water bath; cook for 14 hours.
- Remove the pork from the cooking pouch. Pour the cooking liquid into a pot that is preheated over medium-low heat.
- Add the tomatillos and allow it to simmer about 12 minutes. Add the pork to the cooking liquid along with the sautéed vegetables.
- Allow it to simmer 1 to 2 minutes more; ladle into individual bowls and serve right away topped with fresh cilantro. Enjoy!

---

56. Perfect Pork Burgers
(Ready in about 3 hours 10 minutes | Servings 6)

Burgers are ultimate comfort food but they look far more difficult to make than they actually are! Serve with coleslaw and Dijon mustard if desired.
Per serving: 437 Calories; 29.4g Fat; 3.8g Carbs; 37.2g Protein; 1.8g Sugars

Ingredients

1 ½ pounds pork, ground
3 slices bacon, chopped
1/2 cup breadcrumbs
1/3 cup milk
1/2 cup Romano cheese, preferably freshly grated
2 eggs, whisked

1 tablespoon fresh cilantro, chopped
2 tablespoons scallions, chopped
2 garlic cloves, minced
Salt and pepper, to taste
1/2 teaspoon dried rubbed sage
2 tablespoons canola oil

Directions

- Preheat a sous vide water bath to 140 degrees F.
- In a mixing bowl, thoroughly combine all of the above ingredients, except for canola oil. Shape the mixture into patties.
- Place the patties in cooking pouches and seal tightly. Submerge the cooking pouches in the water bath; cook for 3 hours.
- Remove pork burgers from the cooking pouches and pat them dry. Now, heat the oil in a skillet over a moderately high heat.
- Once hot, sear sous vide burgers, working in batches. Serve the burgers on the buns and enjoy!

57. Oven-Roasted Boston Butt with Mashed Carrots
(Ready in about 18 hours 25 minutes | Servings 8)

Boston butt, also known as pork butt, is the most representative cut used for pulled pork. However, you can roast it in your oven and serve with vegetables. Creamy, velvety and healthy mashed carrots make a great side for this pork main dish.
Per serving: 463 Calories; 19.6g Fat; 49.8g Carbs; 23.7g Protein; 17.3g Sugars

Ingredients

3 pounds Boston butt
2 teaspoons celery salt
1 teaspoon ground black pepper
1 teaspoon paprika
1 teaspoon mustard powder
1 teaspoon dried rosemary
2 tablespoons peanut oil

For the Mashed Carrots:
2 ½ pounds carrots, scrubbed and chopped
1/2 stick butter
1/2 cup chicken stock
1 teaspoon thyme
Sea salt and pepper to taste

Directions

- Preheat a sous vide water bath to 165 degrees F.
- Season Boston butt with celery salt and black pepper.
- Place the pork in cooking pouches and seal tightly. Submerge the cooking pouches in the water bath; cook for 18 hours.
- Remove Boston butt from cooking pouches and pat it dry with paper towels. Massage paprika, mustard powder, rosemary, and peanut oil all over Boston butt.
- Bake in the preheated oven at 450 degrees F approximately 8 minutes, turning over halfway through cooking time.
- In the meantime, bring a large pan of water to a boil. Boil the carrots for about 15 minutes, or until they are fork tender.
- Stir in the remaining ingredients. Mash the mixture using a potato masher. Serve with prepared Boston butt. Bon appétit!

58. Grilled Sausage Tacos
(Ready in about 2 hours 10 minutes | Servings 6)

Get creative and use fresh vegetables to enrich your tacos. In this recipe, you can grill tomatoes, onions or peppers along with sausages.
Per serving: 555 Calories; 42.1g Fat; 14.9g Carbs; 30.1g Protein; 3.2g Sugars

Ingredients

2 pounds natural-casing pork sausage
1/2 cup broth, preferably homemade
2 ounces ale
Ground black pepper, to taste
1/4 teaspoon cayenne pepper

6 corn tortillas, warmed
1 bunch scallions, chopped
1 bunch cilantro, roughly 1 bunch scallions
1/4 cup hot sauce

Directions

- Preheat a sous vide water bath to 145 degrees F.
- Place the pork sausages along with broth, ale, black pepper, and cayenne pepper in cooking pouches and seal tightly. Submerge the cooking pouches in the water bath; cook for 2 hours.
- Pat the sous vide sausages dry.
- Then, grill the sous vide sausages over a moderate heat until browned on all sides.
- Serve warm tortillas with sausages, scallions, cilantro, and hot sauce. Enjoy!

59. The Easiest Pulled Pork Ever
(Ready in about 18 hours 10 minutes | Servings 8)

It's going to be the easiest pulled pork ever! You can finish this sous vide pork in the oven – just add the reserved cooking liquid to the baking dish.

Per serving: 477 Calories; 31.8g Fat; 1.2g Carbs; 43.1g Protein; 0.5g Sugars

Ingredients

3 pounds pork shoulder

Garlic salt and ground black pepper, to taste

1/2 cup broth, preferably homemade

1 tablespoon olive oil

2 shallots, chopped

2 cloves garlic, minced

1 teaspoon dried oregano

Directions

- Preheat a sous vide water bath to 165 degrees F.
- Season pork shoulder generously with salt, and black pepper.
- Now, add the seasoned pork and broth to a large-sized cooking pouch and seal tightly. Submerge the cooking pouch in the water bath; cook for 18 hours.
- Remove the pork from the cooking pouch, reserving the cooking liquid. Then, shred the pork using two forks.
- Heat the oil in a pan over a moderately high heat. Once hot, cook the shallots and garlic until tender and aromatic.
- Now, add the reserved pork and oregano; cook until heated through, adding a splash of cooking liquid, if desired. Serve on dinner rolls and enjoy!

---

60. Butt Roast with Caramelized Onion
(Ready in about 14 hours 15 minutes | Servings 6)

This simple but endlessly crave-worthy pork dish is both elegant and rustic. The secret lies in the simple approach – slowly cooked meat, caramelized onion with dried herbs, and good old freshly crushed garlic.

Per serving: 364 Calories; 21.1g Fat; 2.1g Carbs; 39g Protein; 0.8g Sugars

Ingredients

2 pounds butt roast

1/2 teaspoon garlic salt

1/2 teaspoon freshly ground black pepper

2 tablespoons lard, room temperature

1 teaspoons dried thyme

1 teaspoon dried marjoram

1 teaspoon freshly crushed garlic

1 cup white onion, chopped

Directions

- Preheat a sous vide water bath to 176 degrees F.
- Now, season the pork butt roast with salt and pepper.
- Now, add the seasoned pork to a large-sized cooking pouch and seal tightly. Submerge the cooking pouch in the water bath; cook for 14 hours.
- Then, melt the lard in a pan over a moderately high heat. Cook butt roast, flipping once or twice, until it is well browned. Set it aside.
- Cook the remaining ingredients in pan drippings until the onions are caramelized. Cut butt roast into slices and serve warm with caramelized onions. Bon appétit!

61. Japanese-Style Pork Loin Chop
(Ready in about 4 hours 10 minutes | Servings 6)

Chuunou sauce is a traditional Japanese condiment that includes corn syrup, starch, salt, vinegar, sugar, fruits and vegetables, and spices. Its sweet and spicy taste makes a perfect match for sous vide pork.

Per serving: 442 Calories; 25.4g Fat; 1.6g Carbs; 48.7g Protein; 0.8g Sugars

Ingredients

2 tablespoons olive oil

2 ½ pounds pork loin chop, cut into pieces

2 tablespoons ryorishu

1/2 cup Dashi

2 shallots, chopped

1 teaspoon garlic, minced

1/3 cup Chuunou sauce

Directions

- Heat olive oil in a skillet that is preheated over a moderately high heat. Sear the loin chop until just browned on all sides.
- Add ryorishu to scrape up any browned bits from the bottom of the skillet.
- Preheat a sous vide water bath to 145 degrees F.
- Add the pork to cooking poaches and seal tightly; add Dashi, shallots, garlic, and Chuunou sauce. Submerge the cooking pouch in the water bath; cook for 4 hours.
- Serve warm and enjoy!

---

62. Sunday Pork Shank
(Ready in about 12 hours 10 minutes | Servings 6)

Pork shank is one of the favorite main dishes that cooks perfectly using sous vide method. Pork, honey, and leeks combine very well so this Sunday dish is attractive in appearance too.

Per serving: 435 Calories; 25.8g Fat; 5.7g Carbs; 42.4g Protein; 3.5g Sugars

Ingredients

2 pounds pork shank, slice into pieces

1/3 cup chicken broth, vegetable broth, or water

Kosher salt and freshly ground black pepper, to taste

1 teaspoon caraway seeds

1 tablespoon honey

2 tablespoons grapeseed oil

1 cup leeks, chopped

1 teaspoon dry white wine

Directions

- Preheat a sous vide water bath to 176 degrees F.
- Add the pork, broth, salt, pepper, caraway seeds, and honey to cooking poaches; seal tightly. Submerge the cooking pouch in the water bath; cook for 12 hours.
- Remove the pork from the cooking poaches, reserving cooking liquid.
- Heat the oil in a skillet over a moderately high heat. Once hot, sear the pork on all sides until browned.
- Turn the heat to medium-low and add the leeks and white wine. Add the reserved cooking liquid and let it simmer until the sauce has thickened slightly. Serve immediately. Bon appétit!

63. Rib Chops with Garlic-Mayo Sauce
(Ready in about 6 hours 10 minutes | Servings 6)

If you want to amaze your guests for holidays, give this recipe a try! Serve with sourdough buns, if desired.
Per serving: 475 Calories; 38.2g Fat; 3.1g Carbs; 29.8g Protein; 0.7g Sugars

Ingredients

2 pounds rib chops
Salt and black pepper, to taste
1 teaspoon cayenne pepper
1 sprig thyme
2 sprigs rosemary

1 tablespoon lard, softened
1/2 cup mayonnaise
2 tablespoons sour cream
1 teaspoon garlic, minced
2 heaping tablespoons parsley

Directions

- Preheat a sous vide water bath to 145 degrees F.
- Season the pork chops with salt, black pepper, cayenne pepper, thyme, and rosemary.
- Add the seasoned pork to cooking poaches and seal tightly. Submerge the cooking pouch in the water bath; cook for 6 hours.
- Remove rib chops from the cooking poaches and pat dry with kitchen towels.
- Melt the lard in a pan that is preheated over a moderately high flame. Now, sear the sous vide pork until well browned.
- Meanwhile, make the sauce by mixing the mayonnaise, sour cream, garlic, and parsley. Serve rib chops with the sauce on the side. Bon appétit!

---

64. Honey and Cider Glazed Pork Shoulder
(Ready in about 26 hours 10 minutes | Servings 4)

These sous vide pork shoulder is tender and perfectly glazed. In this recipe, we call for it to be cooked at 145 degrees F. If you increase the temperature of the water bath, you will get a braise-like meat.
Per serving: 520 Calories; 30.5g Fat; 15.7g Carbs; 43.9g Protein; 11.7g Sugars

Ingredients

1 ½ pounds pork shoulder
1⁄2 teaspoon red pepper flakes
Salt and black pepper, to taste
1 tablespoon ghee
1 ½ cups fresh pear cider
2 teaspoons dried Mexican oregano

2 sprigs fresh thyme
1 (1-inch) piece fresh ginger, chopped
1/4 cup tamari sauce
1 tablespoon Miso paste
1 teaspoon garlic paste
3 teaspoons raw honey

Directions

- Preheat a sous vide water bath to 145 degrees F.
- Season the pork with red pepper, salt, and black pepper.
- Add the seasoned pork to cooking poaches and seal tightly. Submerge the cooking pouch in the water bath; cook for 26 hours.
- Remove the pork from the cooking poaches; pat dry with paper towels. Spread the pork with melted ghee on all sides.
- Next, preheat your oven to 425 degrees F. Place the pork on a roasting pan; pour 1 cup of cider into the bottom of the pan.
- Roast for about 30 minutes, flipping halfway through cooking time.
- While meat roasts, add the remaining ingredients to a saucepan; cook until the sauce has thickened slightly.
- Pour the sauce over roasted pork shoulder and serve immediately. Bon appétit!

65. Sunday Barbecue Back Ribs
(Ready in about 25 hours | Servings 6)

In this recipe, we call for back ribs to be cooked at 145 degrees F for a chop-like texture. However, if you tend to achieve chewiness while still tenderizing a majority of the meat, use 140 degrees F. Afterwards, if you prefer a braise-like pork, the temperature of the water bath should be from 156 to 176 degrees F.

Per serving: 378 Calories; 24.3g Fat; 10.1g Carbs; 31.2g Protein; 6.7g Sugars

Ingredients

2 pounds back ribs
1/2 teaspoon coarse salt
1/4 teaspoon ground black pepper
1/2 teaspoon cayenne pepper
1 tablespoon ancho chili powder

1/4 cup brown sugar
1 tablespoon ground cumin
2 teaspoons dry mustard
1 ½ cups barbeque sauce

Directions

- Preheat a sous vide water bath to 145 degrees F.
- Season the pork with salt and ground black pepper.
- Add the seasoned pork to cooking poaches and seal tightly. Submerge the cooking pouch in the water bath; cook for 24 hours.
- Then, thoroughly combine cayenne pepper, ancho chili powder, brown sugar, cumin, and dry mustard in a small-sized mixing bowl.
- Place back ribs on a lightly greased baking sheet. Now, spread the back ribs with an even coat of dry rub. Pour barbecue sauce over them.
- Bake in the preheated oven at 300 degrees F until thoroughly cooked. Serve immediately.

66. Grilled Pork Tenderloin with Chimichurri
(Ready in about 3 hours 35 minutes | Servings 8)

Pork tenderloin is delicious and versatile cut so you can brighten up your weeknight dinner routine easily.

Per serving: 374 Calories; 16.7g Fat; 1.2g Carbs; 51g Protein; 0.2g Sugars

Ingredients

4 garlic cloves, minced
1 jalapeno pepper, seeded and minced
1/4 cup red wine vinegar
1/4 cup fresh flat-leaf parsley, finely chopped

1 lime, juiced
1/4 cup extra-virgin olive oil
3 pounds pork tenderloin
Sea salt and black pepper, to taste

Directions

- Preheat a sous vide water bath to 140 degrees F.
- Thoroughly combine the minced garlic with jalapeno, vinegar, parsley, lime, and olive oil.
- Use 1/2 of this mixture to marinate the pork for 30 minutes. Then, discard the marinade and season the pork with salt and pepper.
- Add the marinated pork to cooking poaches and seal tightly. Submerge the cooking pouch in the water bath; cook for 3 hours.
- Take the sous vide pork tenderloin out of cooking pouches; pat them dry with kitchen towels.
- Preheat your grill to high. Grill the pork tenderloin for 3 minutes per side, until it is well charred. Serve with the remaining chimichurri on the side. Bon appétit!

67. Sirloin Roast with Seasonal Veggies
(Ready in about 6 hours 25 minutes | Servings 6)

A grainy mustard and maple syrup infuse this sous vide pork with mouthwatering flavor, while tomato paste brings just the right amount of tanginess.

Per serving: 489 Calories; 14.8g Fat; 41.1g Carbs; 46.9g Protein; 9.1g Sugars

Ingredients

2 pounds pork sirloin roast
2 tablespoons tomato paste
2 tablespoons grainy mustard
1 tablespoon maple syrup
Salt and pepper, to taste
3 red potatoes, diced
2 carrots, diced

2 stalks celery, diced
2 red onions, cut into wedges
4 garlic cloves, roughly chopped
1 cup vegetable broth
Salt and black pepper, to taste
1 tablespoon fresh thyme leaves
1 tablespoon fresh basil leaves

Directions

- Preheat a sous vide water bath to 145 degrees F.
- Add the sirloin roast to cooking poaches and seal tightly; add tomato paste, mustard, maple syrup, salt, and pepper.
- Submerge the cooking pouch in the water bath; cook for 6 hours. Take the sous vide pork tenderloin out of cooking pouches; pat them dry with kitchen towels.
- Sear the pork in the preheated skillet until it is well browned on both sides.
- In a deep pan, place the vegetables along with vegetable broth, salt, black pepper, thyme, and basil.
- Cook until they are tender, about 20 minutes.
- Dish up the vegetables along with cooking juices onto plates; top with pork, and serve warm. Bon appétit!

---

68. Pineapple and Honey Glazed Ham
(Ready in about 3 hours 30 minutes | Servings 6)

You can add the remaining glaze to the pan drippings; add a tablespoon or two of cornstarch and make a sauce to accompany the ham. Afterwards, reserve the bones and ham trimmings for a nice, homemade soup.

Per serving: 347 Calories; 13.2g Fat; 32.1g Carbs; 25.5g Protein; 25.7g Sugars

Ingredients

1/3 cup pineapple juice
1/3 orange, juiced and zested
1/2 cup honey
2 tablespoons Dijon mustard
1 teaspoon whole cloves

10 juniper berries
2 bay leaves
2 pounds ham steak
Salt and ground black pepper, to taste

Directions

- Preheat a sous vide water bath to 145 degrees F.
- Place the pineapple juice, orange, honey, mustard, cloves, juniper berries, and bay leaves to a saucepan; allow it to simmer for 16 to 18 minutes; reserve.
- Add the sauce and ham to a large-sized cooking pouch; add the salt and pepper, and seal tightly. Submerge the cooking pouch in the water bath; cook for 3 hours.
- Next, preheat your oven to 390 degrees F.
- Roast the ham in the preheated oven for 8 to 12 minutes. Bon appétit!

69. Old-Fashioned Pork Stew
(Ready in about 6 hours 15 minutes | Servings 6)

White vinegar and seasonings help infuse the pork loin with even more moisture and flavor than it normally has. Serve with hot cooked pasta and enjoy!

Per serving: 464 Calories; 23.3g Fat; 10.6g Carbs; 50.1g Protein; 6.5g Sugars

Ingredients

1 tablespoon olive oil

2 ½ pounds pork loin, trimmed and cut into 1-inch chunks

Sea salt, to taste

1/4 teaspoon freshly ground black pepper, or more to taste

1/2 teaspoon cayenne pepper

2 onions, finely diced

2 bell peppers, seeded and sliced

1 serrano pepper, seeded and sliced

2 cloves garlic, minced

1/2 tablespoon rosemary, chopped

1 tablespoon coriander, chopped

1/3 cup white vinegar

1 ½ tablespoons tamari sauce

2 tablespoons fresh chives, chopped

Directions

- Preheat a sous vide water bath to 140 degrees F.
- Heat the oil in a pan over medium-high heat. Once hot, sear the pork loin for 4 minutes per side; season with the salt, black pepper, and cayenne pepper; reserve.
- Turn the heat to medium; now, sauté the onion, peppers, garlic, rosemary, and coriander until the onion is tender and the garlic is fragrant.
- Stir in the vinegar, tamari sauce, and reserved pork loin. Remove from the heat.
- Add all ingredients to a large-sized cooking pouch and seal tightly. Submerge the cooking pouch in the water bath; cook for 6 hours.
- Now, allow the cooking liquid to simmer in a pan over medium-low heat. Continue to cook until the cooking liquid has reduced slightly.
- Add the reserved pork and ladle into individual bowls; serve topped with fresh chives. Enjoy!

---

70. Hot Spicy Sirloin Chops
(Ready in about 6 hours 10 minutes | Servings 4)

Set back and look forward to the incredible sirloin chops ahead! By using a sous vide cooking method, sirloin chops remain succulent and so flavorful that all you need is a fresh chili pepper to make it shine.

Per serving: 340 Calories; 20.4g Fat; 26.1g Carbs; 14.1g Protein; 4.8g Sugars

Ingredients

2 tablespoons cilantro, chopped

2 tablespoons parsley, chopped

1 teaspoon chipotle powder

1 teaspoon onion powder

Salt and black pepper, to taste

A pinch of grated nutmeg

1 ½ pounds sirloin chops

2 tablespoon peanut oil

2 garlic cloves, minced

1 ancho chili pepper, minced

Directions

- Preheat a sous vide water bath to 145 degrees F.
- Thoroughly combine the cilantro, parsley, chipotle powder, onion powder, salt, black pepper, and nutmeg in a mixing bowl.
- Rub the spice mixture on the sirloin chops.
- Add the sirloin chops to a large-sized cooking pouch and seal tightly. Submerge the cooking pouch in the water bath; cook for 6 hours.
- Heat peanut oil in a nonstick skillet over a moderately high heat. Sear the sirloin chops until browned and reserve.
- Cook the garlic and ancho pepper in pan drippings until aromatic. Add sirloin chops and serve immediately. Bon appétit!

71. Roast Pork Loin
(Ready in about 4 hours 10 minutes | Servings 6)

Cooking pork loin roast sous vide has a number of advantages to the traditional methods of searing, roasting or grilling. It comes out moist, tender, juicy, and flavorful!

Per serving: 416 Calories; 21.1g Fat; 3.4g Carbs; 50.2g Protein; 2.2g Sugars

Ingredients

2 ½ pound pork loin roast

1 tablespoon cayenne pepper

1 tablespoon maple syrup

1/2 teaspoon ground cumin

1 teaspoon shallot powder

1 teaspoon garlic powder

Sea salt and freshly ground black pepper, to your liking

1/2 teaspoon dried marjoram

1/2 teaspoon turmeric powder

2 tablespoons lard, at room temperature

Directions

- Preheat a sous vide water bath to 145 degrees F.
- Mix all of the above ingredients, except for the pork. Now, spread all sides of loin roast with this mixture.
- Add the loin roast to a large-sized cooking pouch and seal tightly. Submerge the cooking pouch in the water bath; cook for 4 hours.
- Pat the loin roast dry with paper towels.
- Melt the lard in a skillet over a moderately high heat. Sear the loin roast on all sides until it is well browned.
- Transfer the pork loin roast to a cutting board; slice and serve with roasted vegetables, if desired. Bon appétit!

72. Spicy and Hearty Pork Stew
(Ready in about 18 hours 20 minutes | Servings 6)

This recipe calls for habanero pepper but you can use any type of chili peppers you like. When it comes to the right cooking wine, Pinot Grigio, Unoaked Chardonnay, and Sauvignon Blanc work best for this recipe.

Per serving: 403 Calories; 16.4g Fat; 18.4g Carbs; 44g Protein; 6.8g Sugars

Ingredients

2 pounds pork butt roast, cut into 1-inch cubes

Sea salt and freshly ground black pepper, to your liking

1 tablespoon lard, at room temperature

2 onions, chopped

2 carrots, chopped

2 celery stalks, chopped

2 parsnips, chopped

2 bell peppers, seeded and chopped

1 habanero pepper, seeded and chopped

2 garlic cloves, chopped

2 ½ cups broth, preferably homemade

2 bay leaves

1/2 cup cooking wine

Directions

- Preheat a sous vide water bath to 140 degrees F.
- Season the pork with salt and pepper to taste.
- Add the pork to a large-sized cooking pouch and seal tightly. Submerge the cooking pouch in the water bath; cook for 18 hours.
- Pat the pork butt roast dry with paper towels.
- Melt the lard in a large stockpot over a moderately high heat. Sear the pork on all sides until it is well browned; reserve.
- Then, cook the veggies in pan drippings until softened. Pour in broth; add bay leaves and reserved meat.
- Reduce the heat to medium-low, pour in cooking wine, and allow it to simmer for 15 to 20 minutes or until heated through. Serve with a dollop of sour cream, if desired. Bon appétit!

BEEF

73. Beef with Penne and Purple Cabbage
(Ready in about 5 hours 10 minutes | Servings 6)

You're about to cook the best beef roast you've ever tried! Sous vide is one of the best cooking methods to achieve flavors that will blow you away!

Per serving: 463 Calories; 18.8g Fat; 29.8g Carbs; 46.2g Protein; 3.3g Sugars

Ingredients

2 pounds beef roast

Salt and black pepper, to taste

20 ounces penne, uncooked

2 tablespoons butter

1 yellow onion, peeled and chopped

1 celery stalk, peeled and chopped

2 carrots, peeled and thinly sliced

1 teaspoon garlic paste

2 cups purple cabbage, shredded

2 tablespoons tamari sauce

Directions

- Preheat a sous vide water bath to 158 degrees F.
- Season the beef with salt and black pepper to taste.
- Add the seasoned beef to a large-sized cooking pouch and seal tightly. Submerge the cooking pouch in the water bath; cook for 5 hours.
- Pat the beef dry with paper towels and reserve.
- Cook the penne pasta according to package directions.
- In a wok, melt the butter over medium-high heat. Sauté the onion, celery and carrot until softened.
- Add the garlic paste and cabbage and continue sautéing an additional 3 minutes. Add tamari sauce, penne, and reserved beef to the wok.
- Stir fry an additional minute and serve in individual bowls. Bon appétit!

---

74. Italian-Style Cold Beef Salad
(Ready in about 10 hours 10 minutes | Servings 6)

A long-simmered blade steak with crispy vegetables, fresh vinaigrette and flavorful Parmigiano-Reggiano is a classic Italian recipe that you must try.

Per serving: 306 Calories; 16.2g Fat; 11.7g Carbs; 30.3g Protein; 4.3g Sugars

Ingredients

1 ½ pounds beef blade steak

1/2 teaspoon sea salt

1/4 teaspoon ground black pepper

1 red onion, thinly sliced

2 Roma tomatoes, sliced

2 heads romaine lettuce

1 head radicchio, halved, cored and coarsely chopped

1 tender celery rib, thinly sliced

2 cucumbers, thinly sliced

1/4 cup Sicilian olives, pitted and halved

2 tablespoons mayonnaise

1/4 cup red wine vinegar

1 tablespoon olive oil

Salt and crushed red pepper flakes, to taste

1/2 teaspoon dried oregano

4 pepperoncini

4 ounces Parmigiano-Reggiano cheese, shaved

Directions

- Preheat a sous vide water bath to 140 degrees F.
- Season the beef with salt and black pepper.
- Add the seasoned beef to a large-sized cooking pouch and seal tightly. Submerge the cooking pouch in the water bath; cook for 10 hours.
- Pat the beef dry with paper towels and allow it to rest 5 minutes. Then, thinly slice the beef and allow it to cool completely.
- Transfer the chilled beef to a salad bowl; add the onion, tomatoes, lettuce, radicchio, celery, cucumber, and olives; toss to combine.
- In a small mixing dish, thoroughly combine the mayo, vinegar, olive oil, salt, red pepper flakes, and oregano. Add the mayo mixture to the salad bowl.
- Toss again to combine well and serve topped with sliced pepperoncini and shaved Parmigiano-Reggiano cheese. Bon appétit!

75. Perfect Aromatic Eye Round Steaks
(Ready in about 12 hours 10 minutes | Servings 6)

Eye round steak is tough cut of meat so just go nice and slow. Anyway, for a fork-tender texture, opt for a slightly higher temperature, from 156 to 176 degrees F. If you prefer a cleaner-tasting sear, sear the steaks on the preheated pan without using any oil.

Per serving: 309 Calories; 13.3g Fat; 3.4g Carbs; 44.5g Protein; 1.4g Sugars

Ingredients

2 ½ pounds eye round steaks

Sea salt, to taste

1/4 teaspoon freshly ground black pepper, or more to taste

1/2 teaspoon red pepper flakes, crushed

2 tablespoons peanut oil

1 tablespoon dried sage, crushed

2 sprigs rosemary

1 teaspoon dried basil

4 garlic cloves, smashed

1 yellow onion, chopped

2 bell peppers, chopped

Directions

- Preheat a sous vide water bath to 140 degrees F.
- Season the beef with salt, black pepper, and red pepper flakes.
- Add the seasoned beef to a large-sized cooking pouch and seal tightly. Submerge the cooking pouch in the water bath; cook for 12 hours.
- Next, heat the peanut oil in a pan over medium-high heat. Sear your steaks until browned on all sides; reserve.
- Then, cook the remaining ingredients in pan drippings until the vegetables are tender and aromatic. Spoon this mixture onto seared steaks and serve. Enjoy!

---

76. Must-Serve Beef Meatballs
(Ready in about 12 hours | Servings 4)

You can add a few slices of bacon to this recipe. It gives smokiness and richness to your meatballs.

Per serving: 366 Calories; 19.5g Fat; 15.1g Carbs; 31.7g Protein; 9.6g Sugars

Ingredients

2 tablespoons grapeseed oil

1 teaspoon garlic paste

2 onions, finely chopped

1 teaspoon fresh ginger, grated

1 tablespoon cilantro, minced

1 teaspoon dried basil

1 pound ground chuck

1 ½ tablespoons ketchup

1 tablespoon oyster sauce

Salt and ground black pepper, to taste

1/2 teaspoon hot paprika

Directions

- Heat the oil in a frying pan; once hot, cook the garlic, onions, and ginger until softened.
- Add the sautéed mixture to a mixing bowl. Add the cilantro, basil, beef, ketchup, oyster sauce, salt, black pepper, and hot paprika.
- Mix until everything is well incorporated. Shape the mixture into small bowls.
- Preheat a sous vide water bath to 185 degrees F.
- Add the meatballs to cooking pouches and seal tightly. Submerge the cooking pouches in the water bath; cook for 11 hours 30 minutes.
- Serve over hot cooked spaghetti and enjoy!

77. Melt-in-Your-Mouth Steak
(Ready in about 24 hours 10 minutes | Servings 6)

Sous vide ensures you get moist and tender steak without losing any nutrition and flavor from the meat. Mound fresh salad on a plate and enjoy!

Per serving: 306 Calories; 20.1g Fat; 0.4g Carbs; 28.7g Protein; 0g Sugars

Ingredients

2 pounds flat iron steak

Sea salt, to taste

1/3 teaspoon freshly ground black pepper

1 teaspoon dried marjoram

1/2 teaspoon shallot powder

2 tablespoons lard, room temperature

2 garlic cloves, minced

1 (1-inch) piece ginger, grated

Directions

- Preheat a sous vide water bath to 140 degrees F.
- Season the steak with salt and black pepper.
- Add the seasoned steak to cooking pouches; add the marjoram and shallot powder and seal tightly. Submerge the cooking pouches in the water bath; cook for 24 hours.
- Pat the beef dry with paper towels and allow it to rest for 5 minutes.
- In a pan, melt the lard over medium-high heat. Now, brown the steak for 2 minutes per side.
- Add the garlic and ginger. Cook an additional 2 minutes or until heated through. Bon appétit!

---

78. Favorite Cheesy Meatloaf
(Ready in about 2 hours 40 minutes | Servings 6)

If you're looking for a classic meatloaf recipe that is easy to make, look no further! This meatloaf is great with creamy, rich salad.

Per serving: 437 Calories; 22.4g Fat; 19.9g Carbs; 44.6g Protein; 6.2g Sugars

Ingredients

1 ½ pounds ground chuck

1/2 pound pork, ground

1 white onion, finely chopped

2 garlic cloves, finely chopped

1 jalapeno pepper, minced

1/2 teaspoon dried rosemary

1 teaspoon dried marjoram

1/2 teaspoon dried oregano

2 eggs, beaten

1 cup rolled oats

4 ounces Romano cheese, freshly grated

Salt and black pepper, to taste

3/4 cup tomato puree

2 tablespoons brown sugar

1 tablespoon grainy mustard

Directions

- Preheat a sous vide water bath to 140 degrees F.
- Then, thoroughly combine ground meat with onion, garlic, jalapeno, rosemary, marjoram, oregano, eggs, rolled oats, Romano cheese, salt, and black pepper.
- Mix until everything is well incorporated. Then, shape the mixture into two loaves.
- Add the meatloaves to cooking pouches; seal tightly. Submerge the cooking pouches in the water bath; cook for 2 hours 30 minutes.
- Preheat your oven to 440 degrees F. Now, lightly grease a baking dish with a nonstick cooking spray.
- Place the prepared meatloaves in the baking dish.
- In a mixing dish, whisk the tomato puree, brown sugar, and mustard. Spread this tomato mixture evenly over top.
- Bake for 6 minutes or until a meat thermometer inserted in center of loaf reads 160 degrees F. Bon appétit!

79. Beef Tenderloin in Red Wine Infused Sauce
(Ready in about 3 hours 10 minutes | Servings 4)

Mound a fresh salad on a serving plate. Top with warm beef tenderloin and serve with your favorite side dish.
Per serving: 415 Calories; 17.2g Fat; 8.6g Carbs; 52.8g Protein; 6.1g Sugars

Ingredients

Sea salt and ground black pepper, to taste

1/2 teaspoon paprika

1 teaspoon mustard powder

1 teaspoon fresh ginger, grated

1 tablespoon honey

1 ½ pounds beef tenderloin

2 teaspoons butter, softened

1/2 cup scallions, chopped

2 garlic cloves, grated

2 bell pepper, chopped

1 celery rib, chopped

1/3 cup dry red wine

Directions

- Preheat a sous vide water bath to 149 degrees F.
- In a mixing bowl, thoroughly combine the salt, black pepper, paprika, mustard powder, ginger, and honey.
- Then, massage this spice mixture evenly onto beef tenderloin.
- Add the meat to cooking pouches; seal tightly. Submerge the cooking pouches in the water bath; cook for 3 hours.
- Melt the butter in a nonstick skillet over medium-high heat. Give the sous vide beef a quick sear and reserve.
- Then, sauté the scallions, garlic, peppers, and celery in pan drippings; pour in red wine to deglaze the pan.
- Add the meat back to the skillet and continue to cook until the sauce has reduced. Serve immediately and enjoy!

80. The Best Ever Spaghetti Bolognese
(Ready in about 3 hours | Servings 4)

A well-prepared spaghetti Bolognese is a royal meal. Searing the ground beef in hot oil before cooking it sous vide ensures your sauce stays richly flavored and satisfying.
Per serving: 309 Calories; 15.2g Fat; 10.4g Carbs; 32.2g Protein; 5.6g Sugars

Ingredients

2 teaspoons grapeseed oil

1 pound ground beef

1 onion, chopped

Salt and ground black pepper, to taste

4 ripe tomatoes, chopped

2 garlic cloves, chopped

1 cup fresh basil leaves

1 bell pepper, chopped

1 teaspoon dried oregano

1/2 teaspoon dried basil

1 teaspoon cayenne pepper

1 box spaghetti

Directions

- Preheat a sous vide water bath to 140 degrees F.
- Heat the oil in a cast-iron skillet over a moderately high heat. Once hot, cook the beef and onions for 3 to 4 minutes, stirring continuously.
- Place all ingredients, except for spaghetti, in cooking pouches; seal tightly. Submerge the cooking pouches in the water bath; cook for 2 hours 30 minutes.
- Cook your spaghetti according to package directions. Serve with Bolognese sauce and enjoy!

81. Porterhouse Steak with Pea Purée
(Ready in about 4 hours 10 minutes | Servings 4)

Sous-vide cooking is a great method for preparing any type of butcher's cuts. Actually, a Porterhouse steak is cut from the short loin or more precisely, it is a cut from the rear end of the loin.

Per serving: 449 Calories; 29.3g Fat; 6.1g Carbs; 38.2g Protein; 3.1g Sugars

Ingredients

1 ½ pounds Porterhouse steak, bone-in
Celery salt and freshly ground pepper, to taste
1 teaspoon cayenne pepper
1 tablespoon grapeseed oil

Pea Purée:
8 ounces frozen peas, thawed
2 garlic cloves, minced
2 tablespoons fresh mint leaves
1/3 teaspoon kosher salt
1/3 teaspoon freshly ground black pepper
1/3 teaspoon paprika
2 teaspoons extra-virgin olive oil
1/3 cup cheddar cheese, grated

Directions

- Preheat a sous vide water bath to 144 degrees F.
- Season Porterhouse steak with celery salt, black pepper, and cayenne pepper.
- Place the steak in cooking pouches; seal tightly. Submerge the cooking pouches in the water bath; cook for 4 hours.
- Remove Porterhouse steak from the cooking pouch; pat it dry on both sides.
- Heat the grapeseed oil in a skillet over high heat. Once hot, sear the steak on both sides for 1 to 3 minutes.
- Then, make the pea purée; blitz the peas, garlic, mint, salt, black pepper, and paprika in a food processor.
- With the machine running, add the olive oil and mix until everything is well incorporated.
- Top with grated cheddar cheese; serve with the seared Porterhouse steak. Bon appétit!

82. Easy Fajitas Arrachera
(Ready in about 3 hours 40 minutes | Servings 6)

A hanger steak, also sold as Butcher's steak and arrachera, is an inexpensive cut that is favorite among professional chefs and home cooks. To finish your steaks, use a gas grill or charcoal, it's up to you.

Per serving: 329 Calories; 15.6g Fat; 4.8g Carbs; 43.6g Protein; 1.6g Sugars

Ingredients

2 pounds hanger steaks
Coarse salt and ground black pepper, to your liking

For Pico de gallo:
3 ripe plum tomatoes, chopped
1/2 cup scallions, chopped
2 jalapeno peppers, deveined and minced
1 tablespoon fresh lime juice
1/3 cup fresh cilantro, chopped
1/3 teaspoon sea salt

Directions

- Preheat a sous vide water bath to 145 degrees F.
- Now, season the hanger steaks generously with salt and black pepper.
- Place the hanger steaks in cooking pouches; seal tightly. Submerge the cooking pouches in the water bath; cook for 3 hours 30 minutes.
- Then, remove the steaks from the cooking pouch; pat it dry with kitchen towels.
- Preheat your grill to high. Now, grill the steaks for 1 minute 30 seconds, flipping over every 15 seconds.
- In the meantime, make Pico de gallo by thoroughly mixing all of the above ingredients. Store in your refrigerator until ready to serve.
- Serve grilled steaks with Pico de gallo on the side. Bon appétit!

83. Beef Bottom Round with Honey Lager Sauce
(Ready in about 12 hours 10 minutes | Servings 8)

A delicately flavored lager sauce, with a touch of honey and a hint of spices, makes a great complement to a beef bottom round. Enjoy!
Per serving: 317 Calories; 10.6g Fat; 13.6g Carbs; 38.3g Protein; 10.9g Sugars

Ingredients

3 pounds beef bottom round
Salt and black pepper, to taste
1 tablespoon grapeseed oil
2 yellow onions, chopped
2 garlic cloves, minced
1 bell pepper, thinly sliced
1/3 cup apple cider

1/4 cup tomato paste
1/4 cup honey
1 teaspoon mustard powder
1 cup lager
1 bay leaf
A pinch of grated nutmeg
1/2 teaspoon whole cloves

Directions

- Preheat a sous vide water bath to 165 degrees F.
- Now, season the beef bottom round liberally with salt and black pepper.
- In a large frying pan, heat the oil over high flame. Once hot, sear the beef for 1 minute per side; reserve.
- Then, sauté the onion, garlic, and pepper in pan drippings approximately 8 minutes.
- Place the beef bottom round in cooking pouches; add the sautéed mixture along with the remaining ingredients; seal tightly.
- Submerge the cooking pouches in the water bath; cook for 12 hours.
- Then, remove the beef from the cooking pouch. You can thicken the sauce with cornstarch, if desired. Serve on individual plates. Enjoy!

84. Restaurant-Style Family Cheeseburgers
(Ready in about 4 hours 10 minutes | Servings 6)

Cheeseburgers are a staple for most meat lovers. However, you can make your own homemade burgers and amaze your family!
Per serving: 497 Calories; 29.4g Fat; 19.1g Carbs; 39.1g Protein; 4.9g Sugars

Ingredients

1 ½ pounds ground beef
1 teaspoon garlic powder
Sea salt and freshly ground black pepper, to your liking
1/2 teaspoon cayenne pepper

6 hamburger buns
6 ounces Cheddar cheese, sliced
1 head Iceberg lettuce
3 teaspoons Dijon mustard

Directions

- Preheat a sous vide water bath to 144 degrees F.
- Mix the ground beef with the garlic powder, salt, black pepper, and cayenne pepper; mix well to combine.
- Now, shape the mixture into 6 patties.
- Place the prepared patties in cooking pouches and seal tightly. Submerge the cooking pouches in the water bath; cook for 4 hours.
- Remove the patties from the cooking pouches and pat them dry.
- Preheat your grill to high. Grill the burgers for 1 minute per side. Place them on hamburger buns; top with cheese and serve garnished with lettuce and mustard. Bon appétit!

85. London broil with Elegant Mushroom Sauce
(Ready in about 8 hours 10 minutes | Servings 6)

A sous vide London broil needs just a quick sear to gain a nice crust and amazing taste. Sautéed button mushrooms in a shallot-wine sauce go perfectly on top of London broil.

Per serving: 497 Calories; 29.4g Fat; 19.1g Carbs; 39.1g Protein; 4.9g Sugars

Ingredients

For London broil:
Celery salt and ground black pepper, to taste
1/2 teaspoon paprika
1/3 teaspoon shallot powder
1/3 teaspoon garlic powder
1/2 teaspoon chipotle powder
1/2 teaspoon celery seeds
1 teaspoon dried parsley flakes
2 pounds London broil
1 tablespoons grapeseed oil

For the Sauce:
1 tablespoon butter
1 shallots, chopped
10 ounces button mushrooms, chopped
2 cloves garlic, minced
2 tablespoons red wine
1 tablespoon grainy mustard
1 tablespoon Worcestershire sauce
1 cup beef stock
1 tablespoon all-purpose flour

Directions

- Preheat a sous vide water bath to 176 degrees F.
- Add all seasonings for London broil in a large-sized cooking pouch. Add London broil and shake to combine. Then, vacuum seal the cooking pouch.
- Submerge the cooking pouch in the water bath; cook for 8 hours. Remove the beef from the cooking pouch and pat dry.
- Now, heat grapeseed oil in a cast-iron pan. Sear the beef until it is cooked to your preferred doneness; set it aside.
- Now, melt the butter in the same pan; sauté the shallots until tender. Add the mushrooms and garlic and continue sautéing until aromatic.
- After that, add the wine, mustard, Worcestershire sauce, and beef stock; allow it to simmer an attritional 5 minutes.
- Afterwards, add the flour and cook until the sauce has reduced by half. Spoon the sauce over the seared London broil and serve. Enjoy!

---

86. Pineapple Grilled Prime Rib Roast
(Ready in about 10 hours 40 minutes | Servings 6)

Get ready to a fork-tender meat with a perfectly chewy texture. Serve with a cooked wild rice.

Per serving: 422 Calories; 19.7g Fat; 20.9g Carbs; 41.1g Protein; 19.8g Sugars

Ingredients

2 pounds prime rib roast
3 tablespoons olive oil
1 tablespoon honey
1 teaspoon chipotle powder

1 teaspoon granulated garlic
1 teaspoon mustard seeds
1/4 cup tamari sauce
1 (8-ounce) can pineapple rings

Directions

- Add prime rib roast to a large-sized mixing dish. Now, add the olive oil, honey, chipotle powder, granulated garlic, mustard seeds, tamari sauce, and pineapple juice; reserve the pineapple rings.
- Let it marinate at least 30 minutes in your refrigerator. Remove the beef from the marinade.
- Preheat a sous vide water bath to 140 degrees F.
- Place the marinated beef in a large-sized cooking pouch and seal tightly. Submerge the cooking pouch in the water bath; cook for 10 hours.
- Remove sous vide prime rib roast from the cooking pouch and pat dry.
- Afterwards, finish the sous vide prime rib roast on a grill pan; cook approximately 40 seconds per side, basting with the reserved marinade. Set aside.
- After that, place a few pineapple rings onto the grill pan; allow pineapple rings to cook until they show grill marks.
- Serve the prime rib roast topped with the grilled pineapple rings. Bon appétit!

87. Beef Brisket with Peanut Sauce
(Ready in about 12 hours 10 minutes | Servings 6)

This rich and nutritious beef dish combines melt-in-your-mouth beef brisket with roasted peanut, Thai chilies, and herbs. Amazing!
Per serving: 304 Calories; 22.5g Fat; 5.2g Carbs; 20.1g Protein; 1.6g Sugars

Ingredients

1 ½ pounds beef brisket
Sea salt and ground black pepper, to taste
1 sprig fresh thyme
1 sprig fresh rosemary
2 bay leaves
1/2 teaspoon whole cloves

2 teaspoons peanut oil
1 shallot, diced
1/4 cup peanuts, roasted and salted
2 Thai chilies, stemmed
1 tablespoon fish sauce

Directions

- Preheat a sous vide water bath to 176 degrees F.
- Season the beef brisket with salt and pepper.
- Place the seasoned beef brisket in a large-sized cooking pouch; add the thyme, rosemary, bay leaves, and whole cloves; seal tightly.
- Submerge the cooking pouch in the water bath; cook for 12 hours.
- Heat the peanut oil in a skillet over a moderately high heat. Once hot, sear the beef brisket for 2 minutes, turning over once or twice; reserve.
- Pulse the shallot, peanuts, and chilies in your food processor until finely chopped. Add this mixture to the preheated skillet and cook an additional minute.
- Return the beef brisket to the pan, add fish sauce and stir for 1 to 2 minutes longer to let the flavors meld. Serve immediately.

88. Ribeye Steak with Classic Pepper Sauce
(Ready in about 8 hours 10 minutes | Servings 6)

Make sure to choose your desired doneness before you start cooking: 125 degrees F for rare; 131 degrees F for medium-rare; 140 degrees F for medium-well.
Per serving: 344 Calories; 22.4g Fat; 5.1g Carbs; 30.9g Protein; 2.3g Sugars

Ingredients

2 pounds ribeye steak
Garlic salt and freshly ground black pepper, to your liking
1/2 teaspoon mustard powder
1/2 teaspoon celery seeds
2 tablespoons butter, at room temperature

1 tablespoon mixed peppercorns
1 cup evaporated milk
1 tablespoon fish sauce
1/2 cup fresh cilantro, chopped

Directions

- Preheat a sous vide water bath to 131 degrees F.
- Season the ribeye steak with garlic salt, pepper, mustard powder, and celery seeds.
- Place the seasoned ribeye steak in a large-sized cooking pouch and seal tightly. Submerge the cooking pouch in the water bath; cook for 8 hours.
- Melt the butter in a cast-iron pan that is preheated over a moderately high heat. Sear the steak for a minute or two on each side.
- Turn down heat to simmer; add the peppercorns and milk to the pan. Allow it to simmer approximately 2 minutes
- Add the fish sauce, and continue to simmer stirring constantly, until the sauce is slightly thickened.
- Spoon the sauce over ribeye steak, garnish with fresh cilantro and enjoy!

89. Hungarian Beef Stew

(Ready in about 18 hours 10 minutes | Servings 6)

Here's a recipe for scrumptious family stew you'll never want to be without. Serve with a dollop of sour cream, mashed sweet potatoes or coleslaw.
Per serving: 312 Calories; 14.7g Fat; 9.2g Carbs; 36.3g Protein; 3.9g Sugars

Ingredients

3 slices bacon
2 pounds stew meat, cubed
Salt and ground black pepper, to taste
1 tablespoon Hungarian paprika
1 ½ tablespoons all-purpose flour
2 parsnips, chopped
2 carrots, chopped

2 shallots, peeled and chopped
2 red bell peppers, sliced
3 cloves garlic, smashed
3 cups broth, preferably homemade
2 tablespoons ketchup
2 bay leaves

Directions

- Preheat a sous vide water bath to 165 degrees F.
- Heat a pan over medium flame. Cook the bacon, stirring periodically, until it is crisp, about 7 minutes; reserve.
- Pat the stew meat dry with paper towels; coat the meat cubes on all sides with the salt, black pepper, Hungarian paprika, and all-purpose flour.
- Then, sear the seasoned meat until browned, working in batches; reserve.
- Now, heat the pan over a moderate heat. Cook the parsnips, carrots, shallots, and pepper for about 8 minutes.
- Stir in the garlic and cook until fragrant. Place the reserved bacon, meat, and vegetables in cooking pouches. Add the remaining ingredients and seal tightly.
- Submerge the cooking pouches in the water bath; cook for 18 hours.
- Serve in individual soup bowls and enjoy!

---

90. Rich Family Beef Soup

(Ready in about 18 hours 40 minutes | Servings 6)

This recipe might go on your list of favorite weekend meals. Root vegetables create a burst of flavor!
Per serving: 425 Calories; 14.3g Fat; 33.8g Carbs; 40.9g Protein; 6.8g Sugars

Ingredients

1 ½ pounds boneless chuck roast, cut into 2-inch pieces
Sea salt and ground black pepper, to taste
1 tablespoon tallow
1 leek, sliced
2 parsnips, sliced
2 carrots, sliced
2 celery stalks, diced
2 garlic cloves, minced

2 ripe tomatoes, chopped
2 bay leaves
6 cups broth, preferably homemade
3 tablespoons bouillon granules
1 pound turnips. chopped
1 pound potatoes, chopped
1 tablespoon balsamic vinegar

Directions

- Preheat a sous vide water bath to 165 degrees F.
- Season the chuck roast liberally with salt and black pepper.
- Place the seasoned beef in a large-sized cooking pouch and seal tightly. Submerge the cooking pouch in the water bath; cook for 18 hours.
- Remove the beef from the cooking pouch, reserving the cooking liquid.
- Melt the tallow in a stockpot over a moderately high flame. Sear the beef for 1 minute, stirring periodically; reserve.
- In the same pan, sauté the leeks until tender; add the parsnip, carrot, and celery and cook until softened.
- Now, stir in the garlic, chopped tomatoes, and bay leaves; cook an additional 1 to 2 minutes.
- Add the broth and bouillon granules, bringing it to a boil. Add the remaining ingredients, including the reserved beef.
- Turn down heat to simmer. Cover with the lid and continue cooking for a further 30 minutes.
- Ladle into individual serving bowls and serve hot. Bon appétit!

91. Filet De Boeuf En Croute
(Ready in about 4 hours 15 minutes | Servings 6)

Looking for a festive Christmas dinner idea? This recipe is so addictive, you will make it year after year. Serve with pickles and a decadent sauce of your choice.

Per serving: 323 Calories; 23.9g Fat; 10.3g Carbs; 16.2g Protein; 2.3g Sugars

Ingredients

2 filet mignon steaks, 2-inch thick

Sea salt and ground black pepper, to taste

1 teaspoon mustard powder

1 tablespoon olive oil

2 cloves garlic, chopped

1 sheet puff pastry, thawed

4 thick slices Muenster cheese

1 whole egg

2 teaspoons milk

Directions

- Preheat a sous vide water bath to 140 degrees F.
- Season the filet mignon with salt, black pepper, and mustard powder.
- Place the seasoned filet mignon in a large-sized cooking pouch and seal tightly. Submerge the cooking pouch in the water bath; cook for 3 hours.
- Remove the beef from the cooking pouch, reserving the cooking liquid.
- Heat the olive oil in a skillet that is preheated over a moderately high heat. Sear the filet mignon with garlic for 1 to 2 minutes.
- Roll out puff pastry and cut it in half.
- Add the seared filet mignon. Place the slices of cheese onto center of pastry sheets; fold pastry over.
- In a small mixing dish, make the egg wash by whisking the egg and milk. Brush the pastry sheets with the egg wash.
- Prick top of the pastry with a fork; cover with plastic wrap, and let it chill for 1 hour in your refrigerator.
- Bake at 470 degrees F for about 8 to 12 minutes. Serve immediately.

92. Marinated and Grilled Flank Steak
(Ready in about 16 hours 10 minutes | Servings 4)

This recipe makes a sous vide cooking feel exciting, easy, and luxurious. Consider some add-ons such as angel hair, couscous, noodles, or green beans.

Per serving: 348 Calories; 16.4g Fat; 8.7g Carbs; 38.7g Protein; 5.4g Sugars

Ingredients

1 tablespoons olive oil

1/4 cup red wine vinegar

1/4 cup soy sauce

2 tablespoons lime juice

2 tablespoons soy sauce

2 cloves garlic, minced

1 tablespoon Dijon mustard

Salt and ground black pepper, to taste

1 teaspoon paprika

1 ½ pounds flank steak

Directions

- In a mixing bowl, thoroughly combine the olive oil, wine vinegar, soy sauce, lime juice, soy sauce, garlic, mustard, salt, black pepper, and paprika.
- Add the flank steak and let it marinate for 4 hours.
- Preheat a sous vide water bath to 140 degrees F.
- Place the marinated flank steak in a large-sized cooking pouch and seal tightly. Submerge the cooking pouch in the water bath; cook for 12 hours.
- Remove the flank steak from the cooking pouch, reserving the cooking liquid.
- Preheat your grill to medium-high heat. Place the steaks on the grill. Grill the flank steak for 3 to 4 minutes per side, basting with the reserved marinade. Serve immediately.

93. Blade Steaks with Champagne-Butter Sauce
(Ready in about 10 hours 10 minutes | Servings 6)

This recipe may sound fancy-schmancy but it is so easy to make by using sous vide technique. Make for any occasion and your guest will be amazed.

Per serving: 467 Calories; 32.9g Fat; 1.3g Carbs; 42.5g Protein; 0.5g Sugars

Ingredients

2 pounds blade steaks

Salt and ground black pepper, to taste

1 tablespoon peanut oil

1/2 cup butter

2 rosemary sprigs, chopped

2 thyme sprigs, chopped

3 garlic cloves, minced

1/4 cup Champagne wine

Directions

- Preheat a sous vide water bath to 140 degrees F.
- Sprinkle blade steaks with the salt and ground black pepper.
- Place the seasoned flank steak in a large-sized cooking pouch and seal tightly. Submerge the cooking pouch in the water bath; cook for 10 hours.
- Heat the oil in a skillet over medium-high heat. Once hot, sear the steaks on all sides until well browned; set aside.
- Melt the butter in the same skillet over moderate heat. Add the rosemary, thyme, and garlic; cook until they are aromatic.
- Remove from heat and add Champagne wine. Spoon the sauce over the prepared steaks and serve. Bon appétit!

---

94. Hot Peppery Pot Roast
(Ready in about 12 hours 10 minutes | Servings 4)

Mix the seasonings, ketchup, honey, and red wine for an incredibly tasty sauce. Served with a hot barley and crispy lettuce, this pot roast recipe would win your heart!

Per serving: 337 Calories; 7.8g Fat; 17g Carbs; 51.7g Protein; 10.3g Sugars

Ingredients

1 ½ pounds pot roast, cubed

Salt and ground black pepper

1 medium-sized leek, chopped

2 bell peppers, deveined and sliced

1 serrano pepper, deveined and sliced

3 carrots, cut into 2-inch pieces

1/2 cup red wine

1/2 teaspoon allspice

1/2 teaspoon onion powder

1/2 teaspoon garlic powder

1 tablespoons honey

2 tablespoons ketchup

1/2 cup broth, preferably homemade

2 sprigs fresh rosemary

Directions

- Preheat a sous vide water bath to 156 degrees F.
- Season the pot roast with salt and black pepper.
- Place the seasoned pot roast in cooking pouches and seal tightly. Submerge the cooking pouches in the water bath; cook for 12 hours.
- Remove the pot roast from the cooking pouch, reserving the cooking liquid.
- Heat the oil in a pan; sear the beef for a minute or so, working in batches. Reserve.
- Then, in the same pan, sauté the leeks, peppers, and carrots until just tender.
- Add the wine to deglaze the pot. Add the remaining ingredients and continue cooking until the sauce has reduced slightly.
- Return the meat back to the pan, stir and serve!

95. Shoulder Steak in Cider Sauce
(Ready in about 24 hours 10 minutes | Servings 4)

You can add any additional herbs or aromatics you like. You can also add a few strips of bacon to the pan and skip the olive oil.
Per serving: 314 Calories; 10.7g Fat; 15.9g Carbs; 38.5g Protein; 5.3g Sugars

Ingredients

1 ½ pounds shoulder steak
Sea salt, to taste
1/4 teaspoon ground black pepper
1/2 teaspoon dried basil
1/2 teaspoon dried rosemary
1/2 teaspoon cayenne pepper
1 tablespoon olive oil

2 carrots, sliced
1 parsnip, sliced
2 leeks, thinly sliced
2 garlic cloves, minced
1/3 cup broth, preferably homemade
1/2 cup pear cider vinegar
2 tablespoons ketchup

Directions

- Preheat a sous vide water bath to 140 degrees F.
- Season the shoulder steak generously with salt, black pepper, basil, rosemary, and cayenne pepper.
- Place the seasoned shoulder steak in cooking pouches and seal tightly. Submerge the cooking pouches in the water bath; cook for 24 hours.
- Heat the oil in a cast-iron pan over a moderately high heat. Once hot, sear the shoulder steak for 40 seconds per side; reserve.
- Then, in the same pan, cook the carrots, parsnip, and leeks. Cook until softened.
- Add the remaining ingredients and cook until heated through. Return the beef back to the pan and serve over hot cooked rice. Bon appétit!

---

96. Perfect Beef Chili
(Ready in about 3 hours | Servings 8)

This hearty beef chili features ground chuck and a combo of traditional chili seasonings. Serve with salsa, crushed tortilla chips, or shredded cheese and enjoy!
Per serving: 392 Calories; 13.6g Fat; 33.3g Carbs; 35.3g Protein; 6.3g Sugars

Ingredients

2 tablespoons grapeseed oil
2 pounds ground chuck roast
2 onions, chopped
1 bay leaf
2 garlic cloves, crushed
4 cups broth, preferably homemade

4 ripe tomatoes, chopped
1 teaspoon chili powder
1 teaspoon basil
1 teaspoon dried sage
3 (15.5-ounce) cans dark red kidney beans

Directions

- Preheat a sous vide water bath to 140 degrees F.
- Heat the oil in a cast-iron skillet over a moderately high heat. Once hot, cook the ground chuck, onions, and bay leaf for 3 to 4 minutes, stirring continuously.
- Place this sautéed meat mixture in cooking pouches; seal tightly. Submerge the cooking pouches in the water bath; cook for 2 hours 30 minutes.
- Add sous vide ground beef to a deep pan. Stir in the remaining ingredients and turn the heat to medium-low.
- Allow it to simmer, covered, for 20 minutes more, or until thoroughly heated. Bon appétit!

FISH & SEAFOOD

97. Colorful Prawn and Carrot Salad
(Ready in about 35 minutes + chilling time | Servings 4)

Get ready to a light and healthy prawn salad! Curing your prawns before sous vide cooking will add a touch of freshness, plumpness and deliciousness to the dish.

Per serving: 317 Calories; 19.6g Fat; 36.3g Carbs; 5.9g Protein; 19g Sugars

Ingredients

2 tablespoons sea salt

2 tablespoons granulated sugar

1 pound large prawns, deveined

1/3 cup tablespoons tamarind paste

2 tablespoons fish sauce

2 tablespoons tamari sauce

3 tablespoons lemon juice

1 teaspoon dried thyme

1 teaspoon dried marjoram

1 teaspoon garlic paste

1 teaspoon ginger, freshly grated

2 serrano peppers, minced

2 cucumbers, sliced

1/2 pound carrots, shredded

2 heads Iceberg lettuce, torn into pieces

2 tablespoons olive oil

Directions

- Thoroughly combine the sea salt and sugar in a mixing bowl; add your prawns. Let them rest approximately 15 minutes.
- Rinse the prawns with cold water.
- Preheat a sous vide water bath to 158 degrees F.
- Place this prawns in cooking pouches; seal tightly. Submerge the cooking pouches in the water bath; cook for 10 minutes.
- Remove from the heat and stir until well combined.
- Meanwhile, heat a saucepan over a moderate heat. Add tamarind paste, fish sauce, tamari sauce, lemon juice, thyme, and marjoram; bring it to a boil.
- After that, add garlic paste, ginger, and minced peppers and continue cooking for 1 to 2 minutes more. Allow this mixture to cool completely.
- Add chilled prawns to a salad bowl. Toss with cucumbers, carrots, and lettuce.
- Add the dressing and toss to combine well. Drizzle the olive oil over your salad and serve well-chilled. Bon appétit!

---

98. Cod Fillets with Parsley-Mayo Sauce
(Ready in about 15 minutes | Servings 6)

This sauce has such amazing taste that looks like you spent a lot of time preparing it; actually, it takes less than 10 minutes to whip up this delicious sauce for your fish.

Per serving: 316 Calories; 22.2g Fat; 8.9g Carbs; 22.3g Protein; 0.8g Sugars

Ingredients

6 cod fillets

Sea salt, to taste

1/2 teaspoon ground black pepper

2 tablespoons olive oil

Parsley-Mayo Sauce:

2 tablespoons mayonnaise

4 tablespoons sour cream

1/2 tablespoon lemon juice

1 garlic clove, smashed

1/2 teaspoon grainy mustard

2 tablespoons fresh parsley, chopped

Directions

- Preheat a sous vide water bath to 132 degrees F.
- Season the cod fillets with sea salt and black pepper.
- Place this cod fillets in cooking pouches; seal tightly. Submerge the cooking pouches in the water bath; cook for 10 minutes.
- Remove the cod fillets from the cooking pouches.
- Heat the oil in a cast-iron pan over medium flame. Sear the cod fillets for 1 minute per side.
- Mix all of the sauce ingredients until everything is well combined. Serve the cod fillets with the sauce on the side. Bon appétit!

99. Home-Style Fish Tacos
(Ready in about 20 minutes | Servings 6)

Black sea bass is an excellent source of selenium, omega-3 fatty acids, and protein. In addition, it is a powerhouse of heart-healthy fats.
Per serving: 380 Calories; 8.9g Fat; 45.2g Carbs; 29.1g Protein; 6.5g Sugars

Ingredients

1 ½ pounds black sea bass, 1-inch thick
Sea salt and ground black pepper, to taste
1/2 teaspoon shallot powder
1 teaspoon chili powder
6 corn tortillas (approx. 10-inch dia.)
1 head Iceberg lettuce

1/2 cup sour cream
2 teaspoons grainy mustard
1 red onion, chopped
1/2 cup cilantro leaves, chopped
1/2 cup tomato salsa, preferably homemade

Directions

- Preheat a sous vide water bath to 132 degrees F.
- Season the fish with sea salt, black pepper, shallot powder, and chili powder.
- Place the fish in cooking pouches; seal tightly. Submerge the cooking pouches in the water bath; cook for 35 minutes.
- Warm the tortillas on a grill pan. Divide the fish among the tortillas; garnish with lettuce, sour cream, mustard, onion, cilantro, and salsa. Enjoy!

---

100. Poached Salmon with Portobello Mushroom Sauce
(Ready in about 20 minutes | Servings 6)

A juicy poached salmon and Portobello mushrooms in wine sauce work together to create a splendidly tasty family meal.
Per serving: 283 Calories; 14.6g Fat; 2.9g Carbs; 33.7g Protein; 1.1g Sugars

Ingredients

2 pounds salmon fillets
Salt and ground black pepper, to taste
1 teaspoon cayenne pepper
2 sprigs rosemary
2 sprigs thyme
1/2 teaspoon dried basil

1 tablespoon butter
2 garlic cloves
2 cups Portobello mushrooms, chopped
1/4 cup dry white wine
1 tablespoon flaxseed meal

Directions

- Preheat a sous vide water bath to 132 degrees F.
- Season the salmon with salt, black pepper, cayenne pepper, rosemary, thyme, and basil.
- Place the salmon fillets in cooking pouches; seal tightly. Submerge the cooking pouches in the water bath; cook for 14 minutes.
- Then, melt the butter in a pan over a moderate heat. Sauté the garlic for 30 seconds and add the mushrooms. Cook until they are fragrant.
- Pour in the wine and continue to cook, stirring periodically, until the sauce has reduced by half.
- Add the flaxseed meal to thicken the sauce. Spoon the sauce over the fish and serve immediately. Enjoy!

101. Old-Fashioned Haddock Chowder
(Ready in about 1 hour 40 minutes | Servings 4)

Cooking haddock in the preheated water oven "locks" in the flavors and nutrients. You can prepare this chowder anytime you need a complete family meal.

Per serving: 269 Calories; 10.5g Fat; 7.4g Carbs; 35.3g Protein; 2.1g Sugars

Ingredients

1 ½ pounds haddock, 1.5-inch thick
Sea salt, to taste
1/2 teaspoon ground black pepper
1 tablespoon butter
1 leek, chopped
1/2 cup celery with leaves, chopped

1/2 cup parsnip, chopped
1 tablespoon fresh thyme, chopped
4 cups stock
1/4 cup dry white wine
1/2 teaspoon Sriracha
A few drizzles of extra-virgin olive oil

Directions

- Preheat a sous vide water bath to 132 degrees F.
- Season the haddock liberally with salt and black pepper.
- Place the haddock in cooking pouches; seal tightly. Submerge the cooking pouches in the water bath; cook for 1 hour 25 minutes.
- Now, remove the haddock from the cooking pouches and pat it dry on both sides. Then, flake the fish and reserve.
- In a stockpot, melt the butter over a moderately high heat. Now, sauté the leek, celery, and parsnip until softened.
- Add the thyme, stock, and wine and bring to a boil. Add the reserved haddock to the pot; turn the heat to a simmer; let it simmer for 8 to 12 minutes or until thoroughly heated.
- Add Sriracha, stir and remove from the heat. Ladle into soup bowls and add a few drizzles of olive oil to each serving. Bon appétit!

102. Halibut Steak with Chili Tamarind Sauce
(Ready in about 40 minutes | Servings 6)

With sous vide fish, your festive dinner becomes a breeze! Because this combination of flavors will satisfy literally everyone.

Per serving: 308 Calories; 22.8g Fat; 2.4g Carbs; 21.8g Protein; 1.9g Sugars

Ingredients

2 pounds halibut steaks
Sea salt and freshly ground black pepper, to taste
3 teaspoons butter
3 teaspoons palm sugar, shaved
2 tablespoons tamarind paste
2 fresh red chilies, minced

1 teaspoon garlic paste
1/4 teaspoon ground bay leaf
1 teaspoon capers, drained
2 teaspoons lime juice
1/2 teaspoon smoked paprika

Directions

- Preheat a sous vide water bath to 120 degrees F.
- Season the halibut with salt and black pepper to taste.
- Place the halibut in cooking pouches; seal tightly. Submerge the cooking pouches in the water bath; cook for 30 minutes.
- In the meantime, melt the butter in a saucepan over medium heat. Add the other ingredients, and cook, stirring periodically, until sugar is dissolved.
- Cook the sous vide halibut on a grill pan, basting with the prepared chili tamarind sauce. Serve warm and enjoy!

103. Crispy Seared Bluefish Fillets
(Ready in about 20 minutes | Servings 6)

These pan seared, garlicky fish fillets go perfectly with crispy, fresh lettuce and creamy mashed sweet potatoes. Your guests will be delighted!
Per serving: 212 Calories; 8.6g Fat; 1.2g Carbs; 30.3g Protein; 0.4g Sugars

Ingredients

6 bluefish fillets

Coarse sea salt and ground black pepper, to taste

1 teaspoon dried thyme

1/2 teaspoon dried sage

1 teaspoon dried rosemary

1 teaspoon dried parsley flakes

1/2 teaspoon celery seeds

1 tablespoons olive oil

2 garlic cloves, smashed

Directions

- Preheat a sous vide water bath to 132 degrees F.
- Season the bluefish with salt, black pepper, thyme, sage, rosemary, dried parsley, and celery seeds.
- Place the bluefish in cooking pouches; seal tightly. Submerge the cooking pouches in the water bath; cook for 14 minutes.
- Remove from the cooking pouches and pat it dry on both sides.
- Heat olive oil in a cast-iron pan that is preheated over a moderately high heat. Add smashed garlic along with sous vide fish.
- Sear the bluefish fillets for 30 to 40 seconds on each side. Serve with a fresh salad of choice. Bon appétit!

104. Penne with Fish and Plum Tomatoes
(Ready in about 50 minutes | Servings 4)

A hot cooked penne goes wonderfully with tomato-fish sauce. Garnish with a few sprigs of fresh dill. Serve accompanied by a dry white wine.
Per serving: 600 Calories; 12.1g Fat; 88g Carbs; 39.5g Protein; 3.1g Sugars

Ingredients

1 pound trout

Salt and ground black pepper, to taste

1 (1-pound) box penne

1 tablespoon olive oil

1 teaspoon garlic, crushed

1 (28-ounce) can plum tomatoes, crushed

1/2 teaspoon cayenne pepper

1/2 teaspoon dried basil

1/2 teaspoon dried oregano

Directions

- Preheat a sous vide water bath to 140 degrees F.
- Season the trout with salt and black pepper to taste.
- Place the trout in cooking pouches; seal tightly. Submerge the cooking pouches in the water bath; cook for 35 minutes.
- Remove the sous vide fish from the cooking pouches and reserve.
- Bring a large pot of water to a boil. Cook the penne according to package directions; drain the penne and set aside.
- Heat a skillet over a moderate flame; add the oil.
- Once hot, sauté the garlic for 30 seconds; add tomatoes, cayenne pepper, basil, and oregano. Now, bring it to a high simmer and cook approximately 13 minutes.
- Add cooked penne and trout; gently stir and serve. Bon appétit!

105. Salt Cured Tuna Spread
(Ready in about 2 hours 5 minutes | Servings 8)

The process of curing is an ancient food preservation method. This spread is healthy, rich and satisfying.
Per serving: 148 Calories; 3.2g Fat; 8.1g Carbs; 22.3g Protein; 6.2g Sugars

Ingredients

1/2 cup salt

1/2 cup brown sugar

1 tablespoon black peppercorns, crushed

A bunch of dill, crushed

2 pounds tuna

1 head of roasted garlic

2 tablespoons extra-virgin olive oil

1/3 cup Kalamata olives, pitted and chopped

Directions

- Thoroughly combine the salt, sugar, black peppercorns, and dill.
- Rub the mixture on the tuna; cover and refrigerate for 1 hour.
- Preheat a sous vide water bath to 132 degrees F.
- Rinse the fish and place it in cooking pouches; seal tightly. Submerge the cooking pouches in the water bath; cook for 1 hour.
- Remove the fish from the cooking pouches and pat it dry on both sides.
- Then, using a fork, flake the fish; add the roasted garlic, olive oil, and Kalamata olives; mix until everything is well combined.
- Serve over croutons or toasted bread and enjoy!

106. Monkfish in Sweet and Tangy Sauce
(Ready in about 30 minutes | Servings 6)

By cooking this sweet and tangy sauce along with a fish in the same cooking pouch, you get a mouthwatering layering of flavor in your dish.
Per serving: 232 Calories; 9.1g Fat; 14.7g Carbs; 22.6g Protein; 13g Sugars

Ingredients

2 pounds monkfish

Salt, to taste

1/2 teaspoon black pepper, preferably freshly ground

3 tablespoons olive oil

1 red onion, chopped

2 garlic cloves, minced

1 (1-inch) fresh ginger, grated

1 bell pepper, deveined and chopped

1/2 tamari sauce

2 tablespoons fish sauce

1/4 cup honey

1 teaspoon Sriracha

Directions

- Season the monkfish with salt and black pepper.
- Heat olive oil in a saucepan over a moderate flame. Sauté the onion, garlic, ginger, and bell pepper until softened.
- Remove from heat and add the remaining ingredients.
- Preheat a sous vide water bath to 132 degrees F.
- Add the fish and sauce to cooking pouches; seal tightly. Submerge the cooking pouches in the water bath; cook for 25 minutes. Bon appétit!

107. The Best Ever Seafood Stew
(Ready in about 2 hours 30 minutes | Servings 6)

Here's a healthy, protein-packed soup with fish and shellfish. You'll be amazed how well they turn out when cooked in this way.
Per serving: 273 Calories; 5.1g Fat; 9.3g Carbs; 45.1g Protein; 2.7g Sugars

Ingredients

1 ½ pound clams, cleaned and rinsed

Salt and black pepper, to taste

1 tablespoon fresh parsley

2 garlic cloves

3 teaspoons olive oil

1/2 pound octopus

1 ½ pounds grouper

1 green bell pepper, chopped

1 red bell pepper, chopped

2 jalapeno peppers, minced

10 ounces canned tomatoes

1 teaspoon dried rosemary

1/2 teaspoon dried dill weed

1/2 teaspoon dried basil

1/2 teaspoon lemon rind, preferably freshly grated

3 cups water

Directions

- Preheat a sous vide water bath to 140 degrees F.
- Season the clams with salt and pepper; place the clams, parsley, garlic, and 1 teaspoon of olive oil in a cooking pouch.
- Submerge the cooking pouch in the water bath; cook for 10 minutes.
- Preheat a water bath to 149 degrees F.
- Season the octopus with salt and pepper; place it in a cooking pouch, along with 1 teaspoon of olive oil; seal tightly.
- Submerge the cooking pouch in the water bath; cook for 1 hour 50 minutes.
- Preheat a water bath to 137 degrees F.
- Add the remaining teaspoon of olive oil, grouper, peppers, tomatoes, and seasonings to a cooking pouch.
- Submerge the cooking pouch in the water bath; cook for 20 minutes.
- Transfer all ingredients from the cooking pouches to a stockpot; add 3 cups of water. Now, allow your stew to simmer over a medium-high heat until heated through.
- Ladle into individual bowls and serve.

- 108. Catfish Fillets with Butter-Scallion Sauce
(Ready in about 40 minutes | Servings 6)

Simply add a cooking pouch to the water bath and let it go. Meanwhile, make an elegant and flavorsome butter sauce. Lovely!
Per serving: 229 Calories; 12.9g Fat; 1.2g Carbs; 26.1g Protein; 0.5g Sugars

Ingredients

2 pounds catfish fillets

Sea salt and black pepper, to taste

1/2 stick butter, softened

A bunch of scallions, minced

1/4 cup dry white wine

1 tablespoon lemon juice, freshly squeezed

Directions

- Preheat a sous vide water bath to 132 degrees F.
- Season the catfish with salt and black pepper on both sides.
- Now, place catfish fillets in a cooking pouch and seal tightly. Submerge the cooking pouch in the water bath; cook for 30 minutes.
- Melt the butter in a saucepan over a moderate heat. Now, sauté the scallions until tender.
- Add the wine and lemon juice and continue cooking an additional 5 minutes or until heated through.
- Spoon the sauce over the fish and serve. Bon appétit!

109. Mahi Mahi in Delicate Capers Sauce
(Ready in about 1 hour 40 minutes | Servings 4)

Mahi mahi is brined and then cooked sous vide – it boosts its flavor, moisture and texture.
Per serving: 211 Calories; 9.6g Fat; 4.2g Carbs; 26.7g Protein; 2.4g Sugars

Ingredients

2 cups warm water

1 tablespoon brown sugar

1 tablespoon salt

1 ½ pounds mahi-mahi

3 tablespoons butter, divided

1 small bottle capers

1 lemon, juiced

Directions

● Thoroughly combine warm water, sugar and salt in a mixing bowl; mix until the sugar is completely dissolved.

● Submerge the mahi-mahi in the brine; let it sit for 30 minutes.

● Preheat a sous vide water bath to 140 degrees F.

● Now, place mahi-mahi in a cooking pouch and seal tightly. Submerge the cooking pouch in the water bath; cook for 1 hour.

● In a saucepan, melt the butter over a moderate heat. Add the capers, including the liquid, and lemon.

● Whisk the sauce and add the prepared fish. Serve with mashed potatoes if desired. Bon appétit!

110. Family Fish Burgers
(Ready in about 1 hour 20 minutes | Servings 6)

This recipe utilizes sous vide method to cook the codfish for burgers, making a typically complicated process much funnier and easier.
Per serving: 346 Calories; 13.1g Fat; 32.8g Carbs; 23.7g Protein; 2.7g Sugars

Ingredients

1 ½ pounds cod

Salt and black pepper, to taste

1 tablespoon grainy mustard

1/2 teaspoon fresh ginger, grated

1 teaspoon ancho chili powder

1 yellow onion, chopped

2 garlic cloves, minced

1 cup crushed tortilla chips

2 tablespoons olive oil

6 hamburger buns

2 cucumbers, sliced

2 tomatoes, sliced

3 tablespoons mayonnaise

Directions

● Preheat a sous vide water bath to 132 degrees F.

● Season the cod with salt and black pepper.

● Now, place the fish in a cooking pouch and seal tightly. Submerge the cooking pouch in the water bath; cook for 35 minutes.

● Place the fish along with the mustard, ginger, and ancho chili powder in your food processor; blitz to make a paste-like consistency.

● Add the onion, garlic, and crushed tortilla chips; mix until everything is well incorporated.

● Shape the mixture into 6 patties, cover with plastic wrap and place in your freezer for 40 minutes.

● Heat the oil in a cast-iron pan over medium-high flame. Now, brown the patties for 1 to 2 minutes per side.

● Serve over hamburger buns, garnished with cucumbers, tomatoes and mayonnaise. Bon appétit!

111. Hake Fillets in Sauce with Peanuts
(Ready in about 1 hour 10 minutes | Servings 6)

These hake fillets are cooked sous vide, then, coated in Thai-style hot sauce and served with dry-roasted peanuts for a dish that's refreshing and satisfying.

Per serving: 330 Calories; 20.8g Fat; 13.1g Carbs; 23.5g Protein; 2.5g Sugars

Ingredients

6 hake fillets

Sea salt and ground black pepper, to taste

2 teaspoons peanut oil

1 red onion, chopped

2 Thai chilies, thinly sliced

2 cloves garlic, chopped

3 tablespoons coriander, minced

1/2 cup dry white wine

Zest of 1/2 lime

1/4 cup fresh mint, basil, chopped

2 tablespoons, dry-roasted peanuts, roughly chopped

Directions

- Preheat a sous vide water bath to 140 degrees F.
- Season the fish with salt and black pepper.
- Place the seasoned fish in cooking pouches and seal tightly. Submerge the cooking pouches in the water bath; cook for 1 hour.
- Remove the hake fillets from the cooking pouches and pat them dry; reserve.
- Meanwhile, heat the oil in a pan over a moderately high heat. Once hot, cook the onion, chilies, and garlic until softened and fragrant.
- Add coriander and wine; cook an additional 5 minutes or until the sauce has thickened slightly. Add lime zest and fresh mint; remove from heat and stir to combine well.
- Spoon the sauce over the sous vide fish and serve garnished with roasted peanuts. Bon appétit!

---

112. Thai Flounder Soup
(Ready in about 1 hour 10 minutes | Servings 4)

Try this soup of tropical coconut milk and warm Thai spices. All your senses will enjoy!

Per serving: 224 Calories; 5.5g Fat; 13.7g Carbs; 31.1g Protein; 6.3g Sugars

Ingredients

1 pound flounder

3 kaffir lime leaves

1 tablespoon oyster sauce

3 red Thai chilies

1 (2-inch) piece ginger, peeled

1 tablespoon brown sugar

Sea salt and freshly ground black pepper

14 ounces coconut milk, unsweetened

2 cups chicken stock

1 stalk fresh lemongrass, cut into pieces

4 lemon slices, for garnish

Directions

- Preheat a sous vide water bath to 132 degrees F.
- Place all of the above ingredients, except for lemon slices, in a large-sized cooking pouch; seal tightly. Submerge the cooking pouch in the water bath; cook for 1 hour.
- Remove the fish from the cooking pouch.
- Strain the cooking liquid through a fine-mesh sieve into a stockpot. Bring to a simmer over high heat for 4 to 6 minutes.
- Serve in individual bowls, garnished with fresh lemongrass. Bon appétit!

113. Salmon Steaks with Port Sauce
(Ready in about 1 hour 10 minutes | Servings 6)

Here is one of the best ways to poach the salmon steaks. Fish and seafood cooked sous vide tend to have higher vitamin content compared to those prepared in the traditional way.
Per serving: 286 Calories; 16.1g Fat; 2g Carbs; 31.8g Protein; 0.9g Sugars

Ingredients

2 pounds salmon steaks
Salt and ground black pepper, to taste
1 teaspoon dried basil
1 teaspoon dried oregano
1/2 teaspoon ginger powder
2 teaspoons peanut oil

1/2 cup shallots, chopped
2 garlic cloves, minced
1/2 double cream
1/2 cup port wine
2 tablespoons fresh chives, roughly chopped

Directions

- Preheat a sous vide water bath to 140 degrees F.
- Season the salmon steaks with salt and black pepper.
- Place the salmon steaks in a large-sized cooking pouch; add dried basil, oregano, and ginger powder; seal tightly.
- Submerge the cooking pouch in the water bath; cook for 1 hour.
- Meanwhile, in a saucepan, heat the oil over a moderate flame. Now, sauté the shallots and garlic until softened and fragrant.
- Stir in the cream and wine; turn the temperature to medium-low and allow it to simmer for a further 5 minutes. Spoon the sauce over the salmon and serve garnished with fresh chives. Bon appétit!

---

114. Hot Grilled Tuna Loin
(Ready in about 40 minutes | Servings 4)

In this recipe, the sous vide process infuses the lemon and spice flavors directly into the fish. The result is a flavorful, perfectly cooked and healthy tuna dish.
Per serving: 244 Calories; 12.6g Fat; 5.4g Carbs; 27.1g Protein; 1.8g Sugars

Ingredients

1 pound tuna loin
Salt and ground black pepper, to your liking
1/2 teaspoon smoked paprika
4 slices lemon
2 tablespoons olive oil

2 cloves garlic, minced
1 teaspoon dry mustard
1 teaspoon ancho chili powder
2 tablespoons fresh cilantro, roughly chopped

Directions

- Preheat a sous vide water bath to 140 degrees F.
- Season tuna loin with salt, black pepper, and paprika.
- Place tuna loin in a cooking pouch; add the lemon slices, olive oil, garlic, mustard, and ancho chili powder to the cooking pouch; seal tightly.
- Submerge the cooking pouch in the water bath; cook for 35 minutes.
- Remove the fish from the cooking pouch; pat it dry.
- Next, preheat your grill to high. Grill tuna loin for 1 to 2 minutes per side. Serve topped with fresh cilantro. Bon appétit!

115. Classic Seafood Gumbo
(Ready in about 55 minutes | Servings 8)

How do you make your seafood gumbo epic? Simply use sous vide technique and watch what happens.
Per serving: 539 Calories; 30.7g Fat; 19.9g Carbs; 45.2g Protein; 2.7g Sugars

Ingredients

1 cup vegetable oil
1 cup all-purpose flour
2 medium-sized leeks, chopped
2 bell peppers, chopped
2 celery stalks, chopped
2 carrots, chopped
4 garlic cloves, minced
2 quarts seafood stock
1 teaspoon dried basil

1/2 teaspoon ground bay leaf
1 pound shrimp, peeled and deveined
2 pounds lump crabmeat
Sea salt and ground black pepper, to taste
1 teaspoon hot paprika
1 ½ pounds sole fillets
1 tablespoon filé powder
1/2 cup chopped fresh parsley

Directions

- Heat the oil in a large stockpot over a moderate heat. Stir in the flour and continue to cook to form a roux.
- Turn the heat to medium-low and continue whisking until roux smells nutty, approximately 15 minutes.
- In the meantime, preheat a sous vide water bath to 140 degrees F.
- Place the leeks, pepper, celery, carrot, garlic, seafood stock, basil, ground bay leaf, shrimp, crabmeat, salt, pepper, hot paprika, sole fillets, and filé powder in cooking pouches; seal tightly.
- Submerge the cooking pouches in the water bath; cook for 35 minutes.
- Heat the prepared roux over medium heat; bring to a simmer. Pour in cooking liquid from the cooking pouches and whisk to combine well.
- Add solids from the cooking pouches and continue to simmer until heated through. Serve garnished with fresh parsley.

---

116. Shrimp and Pasta Shell Salad
(Ready in about 35 minutes + chilling time | Servings 4)

Different flavors are balanced at a high level in this refreshing salad, which combines succulent shrimp with amazing vegetables and aioli sauce.
Per serving: 407 Calories; 22.9g Fat; 26.3g Carbs; 26.1g Protein; 6.5g Sugars

Ingredients

1 pound shrimp, deveined and rinsed
Salt and white pepper, to taste
1 teaspoon olive oil
Juice of 2 limes
1 (12-ounce) package small pasta shells
1 red onion, chopped
2 tomatoes, diced

2 cucumbers, sliced
1 bell pepper, seeded and sliced
1 jalapeño pepper, seeded and diced
1/2 cup aioli
1 teaspoon granulated sugar
3 teaspoons balsamic vinegar

Directions

- Preheat a sous vide water bath to 135 degrees F.
- Place the shrimp, salt, white pepper, olive oil, and lime juice in cooking pouches; seal tightly.
- Submerge the cooking pouches in the water bath; cook for 30 minutes.
- Remove the shrimp from the cooking pouches; pat it dry with paper towels and allow it to cool completely.
- Meanwhile, cook pasta shells according to package directions; drain and rinse in cold water. Transfer the pasta to a salad bowl.
- Add the other ingredients and toss to combine. Afterwards, add the chilled shrimp to your salad, toss to combine and serve. Bon appétit!

117. Sardines with Charred Tomatoes and Aioli
(Ready in about 30 minutes | Servings 4)

Juicy and crunchy sardines are paired with charred tomatoes, fresh lettuce and cool, creamy aioli for a protein-filled dish that your family will love.

Per serving: 475 Calories; 32.8g Fat; 7.1g Carbs; 36.8g Protein; 3.8g Sugars

Ingredients

1 ½ pounds sardine, butterflied

2 limes

1 ½ tablespoons extra-virgin olive oil

Salt and white pepper, to taste

1 teaspoon cayenne pepper

2 sprigs thyme

2 bay leaves

2 vine tomatoes

2 tablespoons coarse-grained Dijon mustard

1/3 cup aioli

1 serrano chili pepper, minced

Directions

- Preheat a sous vide water bath to 132 degrees F.
- Divide sardines, limes, olive oil, salt, white pepper, cayenne pepper, thyme, and bay leaves among cooking pouches; seal tightly.
- Submerge the cooking pouches in the water bath; cook for 25 minutes.
- Remove the sardines from the cooking pouches to a paper towel-lined plate.
- After that, blowtorch the skin of sardines and place them on a serving platter. Place tomatoes on a metal sheet tray; use a medium-high flame on a blowtorch to char their skin.
- In a bowl, whisk the mustard, aioli, and chili pepper; whisk until everything is well incorporated.
- Serve sardines with tomatoes and aioli sauce on the side. Bon appétit!

118. Lemon Sole Taco Lettuce Wraps
(Ready in about 30 minutes | Servings 4)

Lemon sole is the star of this dish, so getting it right is the key. By cooking it sous vide, it turns out flaky, super-soft and delicious.

Per serving: 475 Calories; 32.8g Fat; 7.1g Carbs; 36.8g Protein; 3.8g Sugars

Ingredients

1 pound lemon sole

2 tablespoons extra-virgin olive oil

Sea salt and ground black pepper, to taste

10 large lettuce leaves

1 cup cherry tomatoes, halved

1/2 cup scallions, chopped

1 habanero pepper, minced

1/4 cup mayonnaise

A dash of hot sauce

Directions

- Preheat a sous vide water bath to 125 degrees F.
- Add lemon sole, olive oil, salt, and black pepper to a cooking pouch; seal tightly.
- Submerge the cooking pouch in the water bath; cook for 25 minutes.
- To assemble your wraps, divide fish, cherry tomatoes scallions, pepper, mayo and hot sauce evenly between lettuce leaves. Enjoy!

119. Mackerel Fillets with Olive Tapenade
(Ready in about 30 minutes | Servings 6)

Mackerel, also known as Bangada, is one of the healthiest fish in the world. It can boost your immune system, lower cholesterol level, and treat many chronic diseases. To serve, drizzle some extra extra-virgin olive oil over the mackerel fillets and scatter some flaky sea salt over the top.

Per serving: 380 Calories; 23.7g Fat; 3.3g Carbs; 37.2g Protein; 0.5g Sugars

Ingredients

6 mackerel fillets
Salt and ground black pepper, to taste

Olive Tapenade:
4 tablespoons olive oil
1 ¼ cups black olives, pitted, brine-cured

2 tablespoons fresh basil leaves, chopped
2 tablespoons capers, drained
3 anchovies
2 tablespoons lime juice
2 garlic cloves, chopped
Salt and black pepper to taste

Directions

- Preheat a sous vide water bath to 125 degrees F.
- Season the mackerel fillets with salt and pepper.
- Add mackerel to cooking pouches and seal tightly. Submerge the cooking pouches in the water bath; cook for 25 minutes.
- When the mackerel fillets have finished cooking sous vide, remove them from the cooking pouches and pat dry with paper towels.
- Now, make the olive tapenade.
- Thoroughly combine all of the olive tapenade ingredients in a food processor; blitz until the mixture forms a chunky paste. Place in your refrigerator until ready to serve.
- Spoon tapenade over the mackerel fillets and serve. Bon appétit!

---

120. Crispy Curry Cod Fish Sandwich
(Ready in about 1 hour 20 minutes | Servings 6)

The texture of this cod loin is amazing. A brine will boost the texture, flavor and moisture. After sous vide cooking, the codfish is smooth and slightly firm, perfect for these sinfully delicious sandwiches.

Per serving: 430 Calories; 18.2g Fat; 38.2g Carbs; 26.9g Protein; 22.2g Sugars

Ingredients

Brine:
3 cups water
2 cups ice
1/2 cup kosher salt
1/4 cup sugar

Cod Sandwiches:
2 pounds cod loin
2 teaspoons curry paste
1 can coconut milk
1 tablespoon fish sauce
1 teaspoon black whole peppercorns
6 hoagie rolls, toasted
1 head butterhead lettuce
3 teaspoons Dijon mustard

Directions

- To make the brine, thoroughly combine the ingredients in a large bowl; whisk until the sugar has dissolved.
- Add the cod loin to the brine, cover, and refrigerate for about 45 minutes; make sure to turn the fish every 15 minutes to ensure even brining.
- Preheat a sous vide water bath to 132 degrees F.
- Add cod loin to cooking pouches, along with curry paste, coconut milk, fish sauce, and black peppercorns; seal tightly.
- Submerge the cooking pouches in the water bath; cook for 35 minutes.
- Transfer the sous vide cod loin to a paper towel-lined plate and pat it dry on both sides.
- Serve the fish on the toasted hoagie rolls with buttered lettuce and Dijon mustard. Bon appétit!

FRUITS & VEGETABLES

121. Braised Fennel with Peas and Caramelized Onion
(Ready in about 1 hour | Servings 4)

This recipe takes ordinary vegetables and gives them an extraordinary twist. In addition to the amazing flavor, these vegetables have a great texture, which makes them perfect for a side dish or a complete vegetarian meal.

Per serving: 217 Calories; 18.3g Fat; 10.2g Carbs; 4.1g Protein; 5.3g Sugars

Ingredients

1 tablespoon olive oil

1 yellow onion, slice into rings

A pinch of salt

1/2 pound fresh peas

1/2 cup fennel

1/2 cup double cream

1/2 cup broth, preferably homemade

3 tablespoons ghee

1 ½ tablespoons chickpea flour

1/2 teaspoon granulated garlic

1 bay leaf

1/2 teaspoon dried dill

1 teaspoon cayenne pepper

Salt and ground black pepper, to taste

Directions

- Preheat a sous vide water bath to 183 degrees F.
- Heat the olive oil in a nonstick skillet over a moderate flame until it is shimmering. Sauté the onions with a pinch of salt until they are caramelized.
- Add all ingredients, including the caramelized onions, to cooking pouches; seal tightly.
- Submerge the cooking pouches in the water bath; cook for 50 minutes.
- Remove the cooking pouches from the water bath; ladle the vegetables into serving bowls and serve with garlic croutons, if desired. Bon appétit!

---

122. Buttered Brussels Sprouts
(Ready in about 50 minutes | Servings 4)

This dish is flavorful from the vegetables and creamy from the butter. Treat your family to this simple but endlessly delicious side dish.

Per serving: 296 Calories; 23.5g Fat; 19.9g Carbs; 6.6g Protein; 5.3g Sugars

Ingredients

1 ½ pounds Brussels sprouts, halved

1 leek, sliced

2 garlic cloves, smashed

Celery salt and freshly cracked black pepper, to taste

1 stick butter

Directions

- Preheat a sous vide water bath to 183 degrees F.
- Place Brussels sprouts, leek, garlic, celery salt, and black pepper in cooking pouches; seal tightly.
- Submerge the cooking pouches in the water bath; cook for 40 minutes.
- Melt the butter in a large-sized pan. Stir in the vegetables and sauté for 5 minutes, coating them well with melted butter. Taste, adjust the seasonings and serve.

123. Bright Pea Mash
(Ready in about 45 minutes | Servings 4)

Here's a great accompaniment to many vegetarian and meat dishes! It's so easy to make using sous vide technique.
Per serving: 196 Calories; 14.8g Fat; 11.4g Carbs; 5.4g Protein; 5.2g Sugars

Ingredients

1 pound green peas, frozen thawed
2 garlic cloves, smashed
2 tablespoons scallions
1/4 cup basil leaves
1 tablespoon fresh dill weed

1/2 stick butter
1/4 cup sour cream (10 % butterfat)
2 tablespoons pecorino cheese, grated
Sea salt flakes and ground black pepper to taste

Directions

- Preheat a sous vide water bath to 183 degrees F.
- Add the peas, garlic, scallions, basil, and dill to cooking pouches; seal tightly.
- Submerge the cooking pouches in the water bath; cook for 40 minutes.
- Add the contents of cooking pouches to your food processor. Add the remaining ingredients and puree until creamy and uniform.
- Taste, adjust the seasonings and serve. Bon appétit!

124. Root Vegetable Soup with Pita Chips
(Ready in about 55 minutes | Servings 4)

Sure, you can cook a soup on a stovetop. But with sous vide, you get to immerse the root vegetables in a broth and preserve their nutrients.
Per serving: 178 Calories; 7.9g Fat; 23.3g Carbs; 5.3g Protein; 6.6g Sugars

Ingredients

2 shallots, peeled and chopped
2 parsnips, chopped
2 celery stalks, chopped
2 carrots, chopped
1 cup turnip, chopped
2 cloves garlic, minced

4 cups vegetable broth, preferably homemade
2 tablespoons olive oil
2 cups baby spinach
2 heaping tablespoons fresh parsley, chopped
1 sprig fresh rosemary, chopped
1 cup pita chips

Directions

- Preheat a sous vide water bath to 185 degrees F.
- Place the shallots, parsnips, celery, carrots, turnip, garlic, vegetable broth, and olive oil in cooking pouches; seal tightly.
- Submerge the cooking pouches in the water bath; cook for 50 minutes.
- Now, empty the contents into a serving bowl; add baby spinach, parsley, and rosemary. Serve with pita chips and enjoy!

125. Greek-Style Eggplant with Sour Cream
(Ready in about 1 hour 35 minutes | Servings 4)

With tomato puree, garlic paste and a hint of red chili paste, these eggplants are amazingly delicious but they have a little kick, which you can tailor to your taste. Serve with toasted pita wedges.

Per serving: 162 Calories; 8.3g Fat; 20.3g Carbs; 4.7g Protein; 8.9g Sugars

Ingredients

2 pounds eggplant

1/4 cup tomato puree

1 teaspoon red chili paste

1 tablespoon garlic paste

1 cup sour cream

1/2 cup fresh cilantro, chopped

1/2 cup Kalamata olives, pitted and sliced

Directions

- Heat a nonstick skillet over a high heat; blister the skin of your eggplants until they are charred.
- In a small mixing bowl, whisk tomato puree, red chili paste, and garlic paste.
- Slice your eggplants lengthwise into halves. Now, divide the paste among eggplant halves.
- Preheat a sous vide water bath to 185 degrees F.
- Place the eggplant in cooking pouches; seal tightly. Submerge the cooking pouches in the water bath; cook for 1 hour 30 minutes.
- Serve with sour cream topped with fresh cilantro and Kalamata olives. Bon appétit!

126. Sesame Broccoli and Cauliflower
(Ready in about 45 minutes | Servings 4)

A side of broccoli and cauliflower served with black sesame seeds works wonders with fish fillets and fresh mixed salad.

Per serving: 86 Calories; 4.3g Fat; 9.2g Carbs; 6.2g Protein; 2.6g Sugars

Ingredients

1 pound cauliflower, cut into florets

1 pound broccoli, cut into florets

1 teaspoon dried parsley flakes

1/4 teaspoon ground black pepper

Sea salt, to taste

2 teaspoons extra-virgin olive oil

1 tablespoon black sesame seeds

Directions

- Preheat a sous vide water bath to 185 degrees F.
- Place the cauliflower, broccoli, parsley flakes, black pepper, sea salt, and 1 teaspoon of olive oil in cooking pouches; seal tightly.
- Submerge the cooking pouches in the water bath; cook for 40 minutes.
- Remove your veggies form the cooking pouches. Drizzle the remaining teaspoon of olive oil over your veggies.
- Sprinkle with black sesame seeds just before serving. Enjoy!

127. Vanilla Apricots in Syrup
(Ready in about 30 minutes | Servings 4)

When it comes to the fruits, the simplest approach is often the best. Use humble but endlessly inspirational apricots to make this masterpiece dessert for a dinner party.

Per serving: 234 Calories; 0.3g Fat; 60.4g Carbs; 1.9g Protein; 54.7g Sugars

Ingredients

1 cup water

1 cup sugar syrup

1 vanilla pod, seeds scraped

4 cloves

1 star anise

1/2 pound apricots, pitted and halved

Directions

- Preheat a sous vide water bath to 183 degrees F.
- Place the water, sugar syrup, and vanilla, cloves, and anise in a saucepan over a moderate heat. Bring to a rapid boil and immediately remove from the heat.
- Add the syrup and the apricot halves to a cooking pouch; seal tightly.
- Submerge the cooking pouch in the water bath; cook for 25 minutes.
- Serve with whipped cream and enjoy!

128. Simple Apple and Pear Winter Compote
(Ready in about 1 hour | Servings 4)

The only thing better than a bowl of fresh fruits is a bowl of a home-style compote. It is great layered with custard and yogurt or served over baked oatmeal.

Per serving: 226 Calories; 0.5g Fat; 59.9g Carbs; 0.9g Protein; 51.8g Sugars

Ingredients

2 apples, cored and diced

2 pears, cored and diced

1/2 cup stock syrup

1 teaspoon vanilla essence

2 cinnamon sticks

5 green cardamom pods

Directions

- Preheat a sous vide water bath to 185 degrees F.
- Add all of the above ingredients to a large cooking pouch; seal tightly.
- Submerge the cooking pouch in the water bath; cook for 1 hour.
- Serve warm or cold. Bon appétit!

129. Easy Garden Green Beans
(Ready in about 45 minutes | Servings 4)

Here is an easy way to dress up plain green beans for an easy side dish. Sous vide method is an excellent way to cook green beans, retaining their natural, bright green color and keeping the nutritional value.

Per serving: 100 Calories; 7.6g Fat; 8.1g Carbs; 2.1g Protein; 1.4g Sugars

Ingredients

1 ½ pounds fresh green beans, trimmed and snapped in half

2 tablespoons olive oil

Flaky salt and lemon pepper, to taste

3 cloves garlic, minced

Directions

- Preheat a sous vide water bath to 183 degrees F.
- Place the green beans, 1 tablespoon of olive oil, salt, and lemon pepper in a large cooking pouch; seal tightly.
- Submerge the cooking pouch in the water bath; cook for 40 minutes.
- In the meantime, heat the remaining tablespoon of olive oil in a pan; sauté the garlic for 1 minute or until aromatic.
- Add the green beans to the pan with garlic, stir, and serve immediately. Enjoy!

---

130. Beet Salad with Pecans
(Ready in about 1 hour 5 minutes | Servings 4)

After cooking sous vide, your beets are still bright purple and have plenty of fresh flavors. Assemble this wonderful salad and delight your family for Sunday brunch!

Per serving: 206 Calories; 9.7g Fat; 27.4g Carbs; 5.1g Protein; 18.2g Sugars

Ingredients

1 ½ pounds beets, peeled and sliced 1/4-inch thick

1 medium-sized leek

2 garlic cloves, minced

1 cup baby arugula

1/4 cup mayonnaise

1 teaspoon grainy mustard

Salt and ground black pepper, to taste

1/3 teaspoon cumin seeds

2 teaspoons balsamic vinegar

1 tablespoon honey

1/4 cup pecan halves, roasted

Directions

- Preheat a sous vide water bath to 185 degrees F.
- Place the beets in a cooking pouch; seal tightly.
- Submerge the cooking pouch in the water bath; cook for 1 hour. Remove from the cooking pouch.
- Add the leeks, garlic, and baby arugula; toss to combine.
- Then, toss your salad with the mayo, mustard, salt, pepper, cumin, vinegar, and honey; toss again to combine well.
- Serve topped with roasted pecan halves and enjoy!

131. Creamy and Cheesy Kale
(Ready in about 15 minutes | Servings 4)

If you're looking for a light vegetarian dish, sous vide is here to help! Tuscan kale is for more than just salads and garnish.
Per serving: 252 Calories; 11.2g Fat; 29.4g Carbs; 15.3g Protein; 10.4g Sugars

Ingredients

2 pounds Tuscan kale, stems discarded, torn into pieces

2 tablespoons butter

2 shallots, chopped

2 cloves garlic, minced

1 cup half-and-half

4 ounces cheddar cheese, shredded

Salt and black pepper, to taste

1/2 teaspoon cayenne pepper

Directions

- Preheat a sous vide water bath to 190 degrees F.
- Place the kale in a cooking pouch; seal tightly.
- Submerge the cooking pouch in the water bath; cook for 9 minutes. Remove from the cooking pouch.
- Melt the butter in a saucepan over a moderate flame. Now, sauté the shallots and garlic until tender.
- Add half-and-half and bring to a simmer. Remove from heat; stir in cheddar cheese, salt, black pepper, and cayenne pepper.
- Fold in sous vide kale, stir and serve warm. Bon appétit!

---

132. Wine Maple Poached Fruits
(Ready in about 1 hour | Servings 4)

These poached peaches are full of delicious flavors. Believe or not, they taste even better the next day.
Per serving: 294 Calories; 0.3g Fat; 76.1g Carbs; 0.9g Protein; 69.4g Sugars

Ingredients

1 pound ripe peaches, peeled, pitted and halved

1 cup white wine

2 cups water

1 cup maple syrup

1 (1-inch) piece fresh ginger, peeled

1 teaspoon whole cloves

1 vanilla pod

2 sticks cinnamon

1/3 cup almonds, blanched

Directions

- Preheat a sous vide water bath to 170 degrees F.
- Place all ingredient, except for almonds, in a large-sized cooking pouch; seal tightly.
- Submerge the cooking pouch in the water bath; cook for 50 minutes.
- Pour the cooking liquid into a pan that is preheated over a moderate flame. Bring to a rolling boil. Immediately turn the heat to medium.
- Continue to cook an additional 6 minutes, or until the sauce is slightly thickened and syrupy.
- To serve, arrange peach on a serving plate; spoon the wine/maple syrup over them; garnish with blanched almonds. Bon appétit!

133. Creamed Butternut Squash Soup
(Ready in about 1 hour 25 minutes | Servings 4)

For even better presentation, add a spoonful of Greek yogurt or whipped cream to each serving and swirl. Refreshingly easy!
Per serving: 178 Calories; 3.4g Fat; 35.9g Carbs; 4.3g Protein; 6.8g Sugars

Ingredients

1 pound butternut squash, peeled and diced

1/2 pound potatoes, peeled and diced

2 carrots, cut into thick slices

1 stalk celery, diced

2 shallots, cut into wedges

1 tablespoon butter

4 cups water

1 tablespoon bouillon granules

Sea salt and white pepper, to taste

Directions

- Preheat a sous vide water bath to 183 degrees F.
- Divide your veggies among cooking pouches; seal tightly.
- Submerge the cooking pouches in the water bath; cook for 1 hour. Reserve the cooking liquid.
- In a stock pot, melt the butter over a moderately high flame. Add the vegetable solids and water; bring to a boil.
- Add the reserved cooking liquid, bouillon granules, salt, and pepper. Turn the heat to low, cover with the lid, and allow it to simmer for 20 minutes or until heated through.
- Purée the soup with an immersion blender, ladle into bowls, and serve garnished with roasted pepitas. Bon appétit!

---

134. Rosemary Potato Soup
(Ready in about 1 hour 10 minutes | Servings 4)

Savor a creamy vegetarian soup all year long with easy-to-find ingredients. This sous vide soup is guaranteed to become your next go-to recipe.
Per serving: 178 Calories; 3.4g Fat; 35.9g Carbs; 4.3g Protein; 6.8g Sugars

Ingredients

1 pound potatoes, peeled and cubed

2 sprigs fresh rosemary

2 garlic cloves, smashed

2 tablespoons butter

1/2 small white onion, peeled and chopped

1/4 teaspoon ground allspice

Coarse salt and freshly ground black pepper, to your liking

1 cup broth, preferably homemade

1/3 cup double cream

Directions

- Preheat a sous vide water bath to 183 degrees F.
- Place the potatoes, fresh rosemary, and garlic in a cooking pouch; seal tightly.
- Submerge the cooking pouch in the water bath; cook for 1 hour. Remove the potatoes from the cooking pouch, reserving cooking liquid.
- In a pot, melt the butter over medium-high heat. Sauté the onions until translucent.
- Add ground allspice, salt, pepper, and reserved potatoes with cooking liquid. Add broth and bring it to a boil.
- Now, reduce the heat to medium-low; allow the soup to simmer until heated through. Remove from the heat.
- Fold in double cream and stir until well combined. Ladle into four soup bowls and serve immediately. Bon appétit!

135. Herby Braised Leeks
(Ready in about 40 minutes | Servings 4)

You can't go wrong with this simple vegetable side dish. Serve braised leeks over cooked pasta or mashed potatoes and turn it into the main course.

Per serving: 139 Calories; 7.2g Fat; 17.3g Carbs; 2.9g Protein; 4.8g Sugars

Ingredients

1 pound leeks, discard outer leaves and halved lengthwise

1 cup vegetable stock

2 tablespoons sesame oil

2 garlic cloves, sliced

2 thyme sprigs

Sea salt and ground black pepper, to taste

Directions

- Preheat a sous vide water bath to 185 degrees F.
- Place all of the above ingredients in a cooking pouch; seal tightly.
- Submerge the cooking pouch in the water bath; cook for 35 minutes.
- Taste, adjust the seasonings and serve with mashed potatoes. Bon appétit!

---

136. Portobello Mushrooms with Grilled Vegetables
(Ready in about 1 hour | Servings 4)

Good mushrooms deserve the best cooking method. Cooked sous vide with aromatic herbs and served with crisp grilled vegetables, Portobello mushrooms are sure to please.

Per serving: 141 Calories; 8.1g Fat; 13.5g Carbs; 7.9g Protein; 6.4g Sugars

Ingredients

2 pounds Portobello mushrooms

2 tablespoons olive oil

1/2 tablespoon pear cider vinegar

2 garlic cloves, crushed

Sea salt and freshly ground black pepper, to taste

1/2 teaspoon lemon thyme

1 teaspoon sage

1 teaspoon rosemary

1 teaspoon basil

1/2 teaspoon oregano

1 yellow summer squash, cut into 1/2-inch slices

1 red onion, cut into wedges

Directions

- Preheat a sous vide water bath to 140 degrees F.
- Then, simply place all of the above ingredients, except for the summer squash and red onion, in cooking pouches; seal tightly.
- Submerge the cooking pouches in the water bath; cook for 50 minutes.
- In the meantime, place the summer squash and red onion on a grilling grid. Cover and grill vegetable over medium heat about 10 minutes or until crisp-tender.
- Serve sous vide mushrooms with grilled vegetables on the side. Bon appétit!

137. Poached Mixed Berries with Mascarpone Cream
(Ready in about 50 minutes | Servings 4)

This dessert is so cheap but better than many expensive desserts you've ever had. Refreshing berry flavor in combination with an aromatic syrup and a sweet and sour cream is every dessert lover's dream!

Per serving: 202 Calories; 11.6g Fat; 22.7g Carbs; 4.2g Protein; 18.9g Sugars

Ingredients

1 pound mixed berries, halved
1/2 cup water
1/2 cup Semillon wine
1/2 cup apple juice

Mascarpone Cream:
3/4 cup double cream
1/4 cup mascarpone cheese
2 tablespoons agave syrup

Directions

- Preheat a sous vide water bath to 183 degrees F.
- Place mixed berries, water, Semillon wine, and apple juice in a cooking pouch; seal tightly.
- Submerge the cooking pouch in the water bath; cook for 40 minutes.
- Meanwhile, beat the double cream using an electric mixer until fairly thick. Now, add cheese and continue beating until soft peaks form.
- Add agave syrup and mix well.
- Arrange berries and syrup in serving bowls; top with a dollop of mascarpone cream. Bon appétit!

138. Asian-Style Noodle with Fennel
(Ready in about 1 hour 10 minutes | Servings 4)

Cooked the traditional way, fennel becomes dull in color and insipid in flavor. Vacuum packaging them for sous vide improves its texture, moisture, and taste!

Per serving: 471 Calories; 4.6g Fat; 98.7g Carbs; 18.8g Protein; 7.4g Sugars

Ingredients

1 ½ pounds fennel bulb, cut into wedges
2 bay leaves
1 tablespoon sesame oil
1 teaspoon garlic, minced
1 teaspoon grated ginger

Salt and freshly ground black pepper, to taste
1/2 teaspoon Japanese curry powder
16 ounces soba noodles
1 teaspoon Harissa paste
4 tablespoons Ponzu sauce

Directions

- Preheat a sous vide water bath to 185 degrees F.
- Place the fennel and bay leaves in a cooking pouch; seal tightly.
- Submerge the cooking pouch in the water bath; cook for 25 minutes. Remove the fennel wedges from the cooking pouch and pat it dry with kitchen towels; discard bay leaves.
- Heat the oil in a wok over a moderately high heat. Then, cook the garlic and ginger for 40 seconds or until aromatic.
- Stir in the reserved fennel. Cook the fennel until nice and browned on all sides. Season with salt, black pepper, and curry powder.
- Next, cook the noodles according to package instructions. Drain and rinse noodles; add the prepared fennel.
- Stir in Harissa paste and Ponzu sauce; toss to combine well. Serve right away.

139. Mediterranean Vegetable Platter
(Ready in about 40 minutes | Servings 6)

Sous vide cooking is the secret to sophisticated yet easy meals. This platter could be served for dinner or brunch.
Per serving: 101 Calories; 3.5g Fat; 15.8g Carbs; 4.4g Protein; 7.8g Sugars

Ingredients

1/2 pound broccoli
1/2 pound cauliflower
1 pound eggplant
1 pound green beans
2 bay leaves

1 teaspoon mixed whole peppercorns
Sea salt, to taste
1 heaping tablespoon fresh parsley, roughly chopped
1/4 cup tahini paste, preferably homemade
1 lemon, thinly sliced

Directions

- Preheat a sous vide water bath to 183 degrees F.
- Place your veggies along with bay leaves and peppercorns in cooking pouches; seal tightly.
- Submerge the cooking pouches in the water bath; cook for 35 minutes.
- Remove your veggies from the cooking pouch; pat them dry with kitchen towels and season with salt.
- Arrange the vegetables on a nice serving platter; scatter chopped parsley over them. Afterwards, garnish the vegetables with tahini and lemon slices and serve.

140. Harvest Stew in a Bread Bowl
(Ready in about 1 hour 40 minutes | Servings 6)

Many cooks like to cook the winter squash sous vide to guarantee it is perfectly tender. Winter squash is the star of this rich and hearty dish but we shouldn't underestimate the power of sweet corn and beans.
Per serving: 445 Calories; 9.8g Fat; 76.9g Carbs; 15.1g Protein; 11.8g Sugars

Ingredients

2 ½ cups winter squash, peeled and diced
1/2 teaspoon basil
1/2 teaspoon lemon thyme
1 bay leaf
2 garlic cloves, chopped
2 tablespoons oil
2 shallots, chopped
1 bell pepper, seeded and chopped

1 habanero chili pepper, seeded and chopped
Sea salt and ground black pepper, to taste
2 ripe tomatoes, chopped
2 cups chicken stock
1 ½ cups sweet white corn kernels, frozen and thawed
1 (15-ounce) can beans, with liquid
6 round bread loaves

Directions

- Preheat a sous vide water bath to 183 degrees F.
- Place winter squash along with basil, lemon thyme, bay leaf, garlic, and 1 tablespoon of olive oil in cooking pouches; seal tightly.
- Submerge the cooking pouches in the water bath; cook for 1 hour 30 minutes.
- In a large stockpot, heat the remaining tablespoon of oil over a moderately high heat. Once hot, cook the shallots and peppers until softened.
- Add the squash mixture to the stockpot. Add the salt, black pepper, tomatoes and chicken stock; bring to a rolling boil.
- Decrease the heat to low to maintain a simmer; stir in corn and canned beans; simmer for 5 to 8 minutes to allow the flavors to develop.
- While the stew cooks, prepare the bread bowls. Slice off the top of the loaves with a bread knife; hollow out the middle with your hands.
- Ladle hot stew into bread bowls and serve immediately. Bon appétit!

141. Crunchy Apple Salad with Almonds
(Ready in about 40 minutes + chilling time | Servings 4)

Try the best holiday salad ever! Rich and unconventional, this salad will amaze your guests with its deliciousness, freshness and nutritive value!
Per serving: 193 Calories; 6.9g Fat; 33.9g Carbs; 2.3g Protein; 26.8g Sugars

Ingredients

3 crisp eating apples, cored, and sliced

2 tablespoons honey

1/2 cup dried cranberries

1 cup almonds

6 ounces package mixed spring greens

1/4 cup sour cream

1/4 cup mayonnaise

1 teaspoon yellow mustard

1/2 tablespoon lime juice

1 tablespoon sugar

Salt and white pepper, to your liking

Directions

- Preheat a sous vide water bath to 160 degrees F.
- Add the apples and honey to a cooking pouch; seal tightly.
- Submerge the cooking pouches in the water bath; cook for 35 minutes. Remove the apples from the cooking pouch and let them cool completely.
- Transfer the apples to a nice salad bowl. Add the cranberries, almonds, and greens.
- In a mixing bowl, whisk the sour cream, mayonnaise, mustard, lime juice, sugar, salt, and pepper. Whisk until sugar is dissolved.
- Dress the salad and serve well-chilled. Bon appétit!

---

142. Spicy Summer Medley
(Ready in about 1 hour 20 minutes | Servings 6)

This medley is totally effortless to make by using sous vide cooking technique. Your vegetables are cooked to perfection and improved with the best Japanese ingredients.
Per serving: 216 Calories; 9.9g Fat; 28.5g Carbs; 4.8g Protein; 13.1g Sugars

Ingredients

1 pound kabocha pumpkin, cut into wedges

1/2 pound eggplants, sliced

1/2 pound cabbage

4 tablespoons sesame oil

4 cloves garlic, minced

1 teaspoon fresh ginger, grated

2 shallots, peeled and cut into wedges

1 red bell pepper, seeded and thinly sliced

1 yellow bell pepper, seeded and thinly sliced

1 serrano pepper, seeded and thinly sliced

1/4 cup sake

1/4 cup water

2 tablespoons ketchup

2 ripe tomatoes, chopped

Salt and ground black pepper, to taste

1/2 teaspoon cayenne pepper

2 tablespoons miso

2 teaspoons sugar

Directions

- Preheat a sous vide water bath to 183 degrees F.
- Place kabocha pumpkin, eggplants, and cabbage in separate cooking pouches; add 1 tablespoon of sesame oil to each pouch; seal tightly.
- Submerge the cooking pouches in the water bath; cook for 45 minutes.
- When the timer goes off, remove the pouch with eggplants; reserve. Set the timer for a further 20 minutes.
- Remove the pumpkin and cabbage from the cooking pouches; reserve.
- Heat the remaining tablespoon of sesame oil in a pot over a moderate heat.
- Now, sauté the garlic, ginger, shallots and peppers until just softened. Pour in sake to deglaze your pan. Add the water and bring the mixture to a rolling boil for 5 minutes.
- Add the rest of above ingredients, including the reserved vegetables. Now, decrease the heat to low to maintain a simmer; simmer approximately 8 minutes to allow the flavors to develop.
- Ladle into individual bowls and serve warm. Bon appétit!

143. Italian-Style Fruit Toast
(Ready in about 1 hour 20 minutes | Servings 6)

Banana is rich in potassium and B6 while cherries are an excellent source of antioxidants, making them an excellent breakfast staple.
Per serving: 282 Calories; 9.2g Fat; 45.9g Carbs; 6.8g Protein; 37.7g Sugars

Ingredients

1 ½ cups granulated sugar

1 ½ cups water

2 tablespoons fresh cilantro, chiffonade

2 tablespoons freshly squeezed orange juice

1 cup banana, sliced

1 cup cherries

1 cup pears, cored and sliced

2 tablespoons coconut oil, melted

1/2 teaspoon pure vanilla extract

1/4 cup honey

8 slices ciabatta, cut on the bias

1 cup ricotta, at room temperature

1/4 teaspoon ground cinnamon

Directions

- In a saucepan, cook the sugar, water, cilantro, and orange juice over medium-low heat; allow it to simmer about 8 minutes.
- Preheat a sous vide water bath to 183 degrees F.
- Separate fruits in individual cooking pouches by type; divide the prepared syrup among cooking pouches, seal tightly, and let it sit for 30 minutes.
- Submerge the cooking pouches in the water bath; cook for 15 minutes.
- Remove the pouches with banana and cherries from the water bath and reserve the liquid. Cook the pears an additional 25 minutes.
- Toss the sous vide fruit with coconut oil, vanilla extract, and honey. Serve on ciabatta slices topped with the reserved syrup, ricotta and ground cinnamon. Bon appétit!

144. Sweet Potato Casserole
(Ready in about 2 hours | Servings 6)

Here is a holiday classic. Try this amazing sweet potato casserole with a toasted marshmallow topping.
Per serving: 307 Calories; 14.6g Fat; 41.8g Carbs; 4.5g Protein; 11.2g Sugars

Ingredients

2 pounds sweet potatoes, peeled and cut into 1-inch cubes

1/4 teaspoon ground allspice

1 teaspoon vanilla

Salt and white pepper, to taste

4 tablespoons sour cream

1/4 cup butter, softened

1/2 cup finely chopped pecans, divided

2 cups miniature marshmallows

Directions

- Preheat a sous vide water bath to 180 degrees F.
- Add sweet potatoes, allspice, vanilla, salt, and white pepper to a large cooking pouch; seal tightly.
- Submerge the cooking pouch in the water bath; cook for 1 hour 45 minutes.
- Then, mix sweet potatoes with sour cream. Spoon the mixture into a casserole dish.
- Combine the butter with pecans; top the casserole with this butter mixture. Spread miniature marshmallows over the top.
- Preheat the oven to 380 degrees F. Bake for 15 minutes or until the top is golden brown. Bon appétit!

FAST SNACKS & APPETIZERS

145. Baby Potatoes with Creamy Chive Sauce
(Ready in about 1 hour | Servings 6)

What you will love most about using sous vide method to cook potatoes is that you can leave it unsupervised with no risk of it scorching or overcooking. Potatoes are accompanied by a creamy chive sauce that is simple but endlessly delicious.

Per serving: 204 Calories; 10.9g Fat; 23.5g Carbs; 3.8g Protein; 1.1g Sugars

Ingredients

1 ½ pounds baby potatoes

3 tablespoons olive oil

1 teaspoon dried parsley flakes

4 cloves garlic, smashed

1 teaspoon paprika

Flaked sea salt and freshly ground black pepper, to taste

1 cup crème fraiche

2 tablespoons fresh chives, minced

Directions

- Preheat a sous vide water bath to 185 degrees F.
- Place baby potatoes, olive oil, parsley flakes, garlic, paprika, salt, and black pepper in cooking pouches; seal tightly.
- Submerge the cooking pouches in the water bath; cook for 50 minutes. Remove baby potatoes from the cooking pouches and pat them dry with kitchen towels.
- In a mixing dish, combine crème fraiche with minced chives. Serve baby potatoes with the sauce for dipping. Bon appétit!

146. Sweet and Sticky Tebasaki
(Ready in about 4 hours 10 minutes | Servings 6)

Tebasaki is Japanese-style chicken wings. These chicken drumettes are crisp on the outside and juicy and tender inside. What could be better than this?

Per serving: 345 Calories; 23.6g Fat; 6.1g Carbs; 27.2g Protein; 5.3g Sugars

Ingredients

1 ½ pounds chicken drumettes

Coarse sea salt and freshly ground black pepper, to your liking

3 tablespoons packed dark brown sugar

1 teaspoon ginger juice

1 tablespoon sake

1 tablespoon Shoyu sauce

1 teaspoon granulated garlic

1 tablespoon black vinegar

2 teaspoons sesame oil

2 tablespoons sesame seeds, toasted

Directions

- Preheat a sous vide water bath to 148 degrees F.
- Now, season chicken drumettes with salt and black pepper.
- Place the seasoned chicken drumettes in cooking pouches; seal tightly.
- Submerge the cooking pouches in the water bath; cook for 4 hours.
- In a saucepan, heat the sugar, ginger juice, sake, Shoyu sauce, and granulated garlic over medium-high heat.
- Bring the sauce to a rolling boil; add the vinegar and allow this glaze to cool.
- Remove the chicken drumettes from the water bath; pat dry with kitchen towels.
- Heat the oil in a cast-iron skillet over medium-high heat; sear the chicken drumettes until well browned on both sides.
- Transfer the chicken drumettes directly to the bowl of glaze and toss to coat them completely. Serve garnished with toasted sesame seeds. Bon appétit!

147. Baby Carrots with Creamy Sesame Dressing
(Ready in about 1 hour | Servings 6)

Looking for a way to give baby carrots a little more edge? Cook them sous vide and then, serve with creamy, sour and sweet dressing.
Per serving: 129 Calories; 8.1g Fat; 12.8g Carbs; 3.1g Protein; 6.6g Sugars

Ingredients

1 ½ pounds baby carrots
Sea salt and white pepper, to taste
2 teaspoons olive oil
1 tablespoon fresh parsley, minced
1 tablespoon mint, minced

Dressing:
1/3 cup sour cream
1 tablespoon lemon juice
1 teaspoon maple syrup
1/3 cup sesame seeds, toasted
1 tablespoon fresh dill leaves, chopped
1/2 teaspoon mustard powder

Directions

- Preheat a sous vide water bath to 183 degrees F.
- Add baby carrots, salt, white pepper, olive oil, parsley, and mint to cooking pouches; seal tightly.
- Submerge the cooking pouches in the water bath; cook for 55 minutes.
- Now, make the dressing by mixing all ingredients.
- Dress sous vide baby carrots and serve at room temperature. Enjoy!

148. Oven Baked Yam Chips
(Ready in about 1 hour 30 minutes | Servings 4)

Fresh yams, a high-quality olive oil and spices are magically transformed into a healthy and flavorful snack that your family will love!
Per serving: 193 Calories; 6.9g Fat; 31.6g Carbs; 1.8g Protein; 0.6g Sugars

Ingredients

1 pound yams, peeled and cubed
Coarse sea salt and freshly ground black pepper, to taste
2 tablespoons extra-virgin olive oil

1/2 teaspoon Hungarian paprika
1/3 teaspoon ancho chili powder

Directions

- Preheat a sous vide water bath to 183 degrees F.
- Season the yams with salt and pepper.
- Add the yams to a cooking pouch; seal tightly.
- Submerge the cooking pouch in the water bath; cook for 60 minutes. Remove the yams from the cooking pouch and pat them dry.
- Preheat an oven to 350 degrees F. Arrange the yams on a parchment-lined baking sheet in a single layer.
- Drizzle olive oil over sous vide yams; sprinkle Hungarian paprika and ancho chili powder over them.
- Bake approximately 25 minutes. Bon appétit!

149. Delicious Traditional Hummus
(Ready in about 3 hours 15 minutes | Servings 12)

If you want to make hummus from scratch, sous vide is here to help. This is the perfect dip for any occasion.
Per serving: 225 Calories; 9.6g Fat; 27.2g Carbs; 9.6g Protein; 4.6g Sugars

Ingredients

1 pound chickpeas

1/3 cup fresh lemon juice

1/2 cup tahini, see our homemade tahini recipe

2 garlic cloves, smashed

1 teaspoon onion powder

1 teaspoon cayenne pepper

Salt and black pepper, to taste

1/4 cup extra-virgin olive oil

Directions

- Add your chickpeas to a large-sized bowl; cover with several inches of water. Soak chickpeas in water overnight.
- Strain chickpeas and discard water.
- Preheat a sous vide water bath to 183 degrees F.
- Add chickpeas along with 4 cups of water to a large-sized cooking pouch; seal tightly.
- Submerge the cooking pouch in the water bath; cook for 3 hours 10 minutes.
- Add sous vide chickpeas to your food processor. Now, add the remaining ingredients and mix until everything is well incorporated. Serve well chilled. Bon appétit!

150. Skinny Sweet Potato Fries
(Ready in about 1 hour 15 minutes | Servings 4)

Healthy snack seems a lot harder to make than it actually is. Try these fries for an easy and nutritious movie night snack.
Per serving: 134 Calories; 7.8g Fat; 15.1g Carbs; 4.2g Protein; 0g Sugars

Ingredients

1 ½ pounds sweet potatoes, peeled and cut into sticks

1 cup water

1 tablespoon sea salt

1/4 teaspoon ground allspice

2 tablespoons canola oil

Directions

- Preheat a sous vide water bath to 183 degrees F.
- Add sweet potatoes, water, salt, and allspice to cooking pouches; seal tightly.
- Submerge the cooking pouches in the water bath; cook for 60 minutes. Pat dry sweet potatoes.
- In a bowl, toss sweet potatoes with canola oil. Arrange sweet potatoes on a parchment-lined baking sheet.
- Preheat an oven to 400 degrees F. Bake for 10 minutes or until nice and crisp. Serve with your favorite sauce for dipping. Enjoy!

151. Asparagus with Garlic Dipping Sauce
(Ready in about 40 minutes | Servings 8)

If you like garlic you will love this appetizer. It's so easy and fun to prepare the best food for the big game.
Per serving: 232 Calories; 19.5g Fat; 9.9g Carbs; 6.2g Protein; 3.7g Sugars

Ingredients

1 ½ pounds asparagus spears, halved lengthwise

1/2 stick butter, melted

Sea salt and black pepper, to taste

4 garlic cloves, minced

1/2 cup plain yogurt

1/4 cup sour cream

1/4 cup mayonnaise

10 garlic cloves, smashed

Salt and pepper, to taste

Directions

- Preheat a sous vide water bath to 183 degrees F.
- Place asparagus spears, butter, salt, black pepper, and 4 garlic cloves in a large-sized cooking pouch; seal tightly.
- Submerge the cooking pouch in the water bath; cook for 30 minutes.
- In a bowl, mix the remaining ingredients to prepare a dipping sauce. Serve asparagus with garlic dipping sauce and enjoy!

---

152. Herby and Garlicky Corn on the Cob
(Ready in about 30 minutes | Servings 6)

Sous vide ensures that you get perfectly cooked corn on the cob every time. You can tailor this sous vide corn on the cob to your preference by adding or skipping some spices. You can also add a melted yellow cheese, salsa or guacamole.
Per serving: 397 Calories; 31.7g Fat; 30.2g Carbs; 4.6g Protein; 0.2g Sugars

Ingredients

2 sticks butter, melted

1 tablespoon paprika

1 tablespoon fresh chives, chopped

1 teaspoon granulated garlic

1 teaspoon shallot powder

6 ears corn

Flaked sea salt and white pepper, to taste

Directions

- Preheat a sous vide water bath to 183 degrees F.
- Toss corn on the cob with all ingredients.
- Place the seasoned corn in cooking pouches; seal tightly.
- Submerge the cooking pouches in the water bath; cook for 25 minutes.
- Taste, adjust the seasonings, and serve right away. Bon appétit!

153. Delicious Artichokes with Simple Dip
(Ready in about 1 hour | Servings 6)

Many people get put off cooking artichokes because they find it difficult to prepare. This artichoke recipe is simple, yet powerful snack.
Per serving: 314 Calories; 24.1g Fat; 20.1g Carbs; 8.3g Protein; 1.9g Sugars

Ingredients

6 artichokes, trimmed and cut into halves
1 ½ sticks butter, room temperature
6 cloves garlic, peeled
2 teaspoons lemon zest
Sea salt and freshly ground black pepper, to taste
1/2 cup sour cream
1/2 cup mayonnaise

Directions

- Preheat a sous vide water bath to 183 degrees F.
- Place trimmed artichokes along with butter, garlic, lemon zest, salt and black pepper in cooking pouches; seal tightly.
- Submerge the cooking pouches in the water bath; cook for 50 minutes. Remove artichokes from the water bath and pat them dry. Then, blow torch artichokes to get the char marks.
- Place artichokes on a serving platter.
- In a bowl, mix the sour cream and mayonnaise. Serve artichokes with sour cream-mayo dip on the side. Bon appétit!

---

154. Traditional French Béarnaise Sauce
(Ready in about 45 minutes | Servings 12)

This traditional French sauce is elegant, delicious, and versatile. When it comes to the snacks and appetizers, use it to stuff deviled eggs, spoon over chicken wigs or vegetable bites and so forth.
Per serving: 175 Calories; 18.2g Fat; 1g Carbs; 2.4g Protein; 0.3g Sugars

Ingredients

4 tablespoons Champagne vinegar
1/2 cup dry white wine
1 tablespoon fresh tarragon, finely chopped
3 tablespoons shallots, finely chopped
5 egg yolks
2 sticks butter, melted
1 tablespoon fresh lemon juice

Directions

- Preheat a sous vide water bath to 148 degrees F.
- In a pan, place the vinegar, wine, tarragon, and shallots; bring to a rolling boil.
- Turn down heat to simmer. Continue cooking for 12 minutes.
- Strain the mixture through a fine-mesh strainer into a food processor. Fold in the egg yolks and blitz mixture until uniform and smooth.
- Place the sauce in cooking pouches; seal tightly. Submerge the cooking pouches in the water bath; cook for 25 minutes.
- Add the contents from the cooking pouches to a mixing dish; add the butter and lemon juice; mix with an immersion blender until smooth.
- Serve with your favorite roasted vegetable bites. Bon appétit!

155. Kale Two-Cheese Dip
(Ready in about 50 minutes | Servings 10)

This creamy sauce combines amazing flavors of two kinds of cheese, ale, and Thai fish sauce. With fresh kale leaves and garlic, this sauce is rich and flavorful, and with a hint of Thai chili pepper, spicy as well.
Per serving: 79 Calories; 4.6g Fat; 3.8g Carbs; 5.7g Protein; 3.1g Sugars

Ingredients

1/2 pound Cottage cheese
4 ounces Colby cheese, shredded
1 cup ale
1/4 cup Thai fish sauce
1 cup kale leaves, chopped

2 garlic cloves, smashed
1 sun-dried Thai chili, finely chopped
1 teaspoon mustard powder
Sea salt and ground black pepper, to taste

Directions

- Preheat a sous vide water bath to 183 degrees F.
- Place all ingredients in cooking pouches; seal tightly.
- Submerge the cooking pouches in the water bath; cook for 45 minutes.
- Serve with tortilla chips, breadsticks or veggie chips. Enjoy!

---

156. Dinner Party Country-Style Ribs
(Ready in about 18 hours 25 minutes | Servings 10)

Pork ribs can inspire us in so many ways! In this sous vide recipe, they're coated with sweet, sticky sauce with seasonings.
Per serving: 280 Calories; 8.9g Fat; 7.3g Carbs; 40.2g Protein; 5.3g Sugars

Ingredients

4 pounds country-style ribs
1 cup stock, preferably homemade
1 teaspoon mustard powder
1/2 teaspoon onion powder
1/2 teaspoon garlic powder

1/2 cup brown sugar, packed
2 tablespoons arrowroot powder
1/2 teaspoon ground ginger
1/3 cup tamari sauce

Directions

- Preheat a sous vide water bath to 145 degrees F.
- Place ribs, stock, mustard powder, onion powder, and garlic powder in cooking pouches; seal tightly.
- Submerge the cooking pouches in the water bath; cook for 18 hours.
- Preheat an oven to 360 degrees F. Place sous vide ribs along with cooking liquid in a baking pan.
- In a mixing dish, whisk the sugar, arrowroot, ground ginger, and tamari sauce. Pour the sauce over the ribs.
- Bake the ribs, turning once or twice, for 20 minutes or until they're crisped. Enjoy!

157. Classic Cocktail Meatballs
(Ready in about 3 hours 10 minutes | Servings 10)

These party meatballs are juicy, spicy and flavorful. Sure, you can add a small amount of ancho chili powder to the meatballs, but feel free to leave it out.

Per serving: 276 Calories; 15.8g Fat; 7.7g Carbs; 24.4g Protein; 1.2g Sugars

Ingredients

1 pound ground beef
1/2 pound ground pork
1/2 pound mild sausage, ground
2 eggs
1/2 cup seasoned breadcrumbs
1 cup leeks, finely chopped

1 teaspoon garlic paste
1/4 teaspoon ground allspice
1/2 teaspoon ancho chili powder
1/2 teaspoon dried marjoram
1 teaspoon dried basil
Salt and ground black pepper, to taste

Directions

- Preheat a sous vide water bath to 145 degrees F.
- Thoroughly combine all ingredients in a mixing bowl. Shape the mixture into small, bite-sized balls (you can use an ice cream scoop).
- Place the meatballs in cooking pouches; seal tightly.
- Submerge the cooking pouches in the water bath; cook for 3 hours.
- Spritz a nonstick cooking spray in a cast-iron pan. Sear the meatballs for 2 to 3 minutes, working in batches. Serve with toothpicks and napkins. Bon appétit!

158. Kielbasa Bites in Beer and Apple Jelly Sauce
(Ready in about 2 hours 5 minutes | Servings 12)

Here's a smart way to use kielbasa, the famous Polish sausage. This appetizer will become a hit among your guests!

Per serving: 241 Calories; 18.2g Fat; 6.5g Carbs; 13.1g Protein; 1.7g Sugars

Ingredients

2 ½ pounds kielbasa, cut into 1/2-inch thick slices
4 ounces lager beer
2 bay leaves

1 teaspoon mixed whole peppercorns
1 (18-ounce) jar apple jelly
2 tablespoons spicy brown mustard

Directions

- Preheat a sous vide water bath to 150 degrees F.
- Place kielbasa, beer, bay leaves, and peppercorns in cooking pouches; add apple jelly and mustard; seal tightly.
- Submerge the cooking pouches in the water bath; cook for 2 hours. Serve with cocktail sticks.

159. Cheesy and Crispy Polenta Squares
(Ready in about 2 hours 20 minutes | Servings 6)

Need a last-minute appetizer for a family gathering? Serve these polenta squares and have a great time with your family!
Per serving: 225 Calories; 19.2g Fat; 8.1g Carbs; 5.1g Protein; 0.3g Sugars

Ingredients

1/2 pound polenta

2 cups water

2 cups broth, preferably homemade

1 stick butter, diced

1/2 cup Monterey-Jack cheese, freshly grated

Salt and pepper, to taste

1 teaspoon paprika

Directions

- Preheat a sous vide water bath to 185 degrees F.
- Add the polenta, water, broth and butter to cooking pouches; seal tightly.
- Submerge the cooking pouches in the water bath; cook for 2 hours 10 minutes.
- Place sous vide polenta in a mixing bowl. Add shredded cheese, salt, pepper, and paprika; stir to combine well. Spoon the polenta into a baking pan; cover and chill overnight.
- Cut polenta into squares and spritz with a nonstick cooking spray.
- Place under a preheated broiler for 6 to 7 minutes, flipping halfway through. You can top polenta squares with some extra cheese if desired. Bon appétit!

---

160. Cheesy Taco Dip
(Ready in about 2 hours 5 minutes | Servings 10)

This dipping sauce is rich and delicious, yet so fun and easy to prepare. If you don't have Taco seasoning on hand, you can make your own blend by mixing chili powder, paprika, ground cumin, oregano, onion powder, and ground black pepper.
Per serving: 195 Calories; 10.2g Fat; 4.7g Carbs; 20.4g Protein; 2g Sugars

Ingredients

1 pound pork, ground

1/2 pound beef, ground

1 teaspoon Taco seasoning

1/2 cup medium-hot taco sauce

1 cup shallots, chopped

3 garlic cloves, chopped

12 ounces cream of celery soup

1 cup processed American cheese

Sea salt and ground black pepper, to taste

Directions

- Preheat a sous vide water bath to 140 degrees F.
- Place all ingredients in cooking pouches; seal tightly.
- Submerge the cooking pouches in the water bath; cook for 2 hours.
- Season, adjust the seasonings and serve with veggie sticks or tortilla chips. Enjoy!

161. Luxury and Rich French Fondue
(Ready in about 40 minutes | Servings 12)

Here's the recipe for a smooth and rich fondue, the star of every party! Serve with your favorite morsels like pieces of good quality artisan bread.

Per serving: 191 Calories; 12.4g Fat; 6.3g Carbs; 13.6g Protein; 2.4g Sugars

Ingredients

1 clove garlic, cut in half
1 cup dry white wine
12 ounces Swiss cheese, shredded
12 ounces Cheddar cheese
3 tablespoons flour

3 tablespoons Kirsch
1/4 teaspoon freshly grated nutmeg
A pinch of paprika
Salt and ground black pepper, to taste

Directions

- Preheat a sous vide water bath to 170 degrees F.
- Rub the inside of a pan with the garlic halves. In the pan, cook wine over a high heat; bring to a boil and turn the heat to medium-low.
- In a mixing bowl, combine cheeses and flour; now, gradually stir this mixture into the wine.
- Continue cooking until cheese is melted completely. Transfer this mixture to cooking pouches; add the remaining ingredients and seal tightly.
- Submerge the cooking pouches in the water bath; cook for 35 minutes.
- Pour your fondue into a warm serving bowl and serve immediately.

---

162. Pickled Pineapple Salsa
(Ready in about 40 minutes | Servings 4)

A sous vide water bath makes a homemade pickled pineapple easily and effortlessly. You may need to adjust the number of jalapeno chili peppers according to your personal preferences.

Per serving: 58 Calories; 0.2g Fat; 15.3g Carbs; 0.7g Protein; 11.4g Sugars

Ingredients

1/2 pineapple, peeled, cored and chopped
1 red onion, sliced
1 jalapeno pepper, stemmed, seeded and finely chopped
1/3 cup white distilled vinegar
1/2 teaspoon coriander seeds
1/2 teaspoon mustard seed

1/2 teaspoon whole allspice
2 whole cloves
1/2 teaspoon ground ginger
1 bay leaf, crumbled
1 cinnamon stick
Kosher salt and freshly ground black pepper, to taste

Directions

- Preheat a sous vide water bath to 145 degrees F.
- Divide all ingredients among cooking pouches and seal tightly.
- Submerge the cooking pouches in the water bath; cook for 35 minutes.
- Remove the contents of the cooking pouches to a bowl and let it cool down fully. Store in a clean glass jar for up to a week. Enjoy!

163. Rich and Easy Pizza Dip
(Ready in about 3 hours 20 minutes | Servings 12)

Looking for a special dip for the next game day? Dig into a warm bowl of this cheesy goodness and enjoy!
Per serving: 230 Calories; 16.7g Fat; 3.4g Carbs; 16.4g Protein; 1.8g Sugars

Ingredients

10 ounces Cottage cheese, at room temperature

2 cups Colby cheese, freshly grated

1 cup Romano cheese, shredded

3/4 cup pasta sauce

1/2 teaspoon dried parsley

1/2 teaspoon dried basil

1/2 pound ground pork

1 ounce pepperoni, sliced

2 tablespoons green pepper, chopped

1/4 cup black olives, sliced

Directions

- Preheat a sous vide water bath to 145 degrees F.
- Divide all ingredients among cooking pouches, except for Colby cheese; seal tightly.
- Submerge the cooking pouches in the water bath; cook for 3 hours.
- Preheat your oven to 380 degrees F. Spritz a pie dish with a nonstick cooking spray. Transfer the contents of cooking pouches to the prepared pie dish.
- Top with a freshly grated Colby cheese.
- Bake for 15 minutes or until it is done to your liking. Bon appétit!

---

164. Party-Friendly Mini Sliders
(Ready in about 3 hours 15 minutes | Servings 8)

These small burgers with Gorgonzola cheese are great for serving a crowd. They are super versatile and take under 10 minutes to assemble.
Per serving: 314 Calories; 20.4g Fat; 10.8g Carbs; 21.6g Protein; 3.5g Sugars

Ingredients

1/2 pound ground pork

1/2 pound ground sirloin

Sea salt and freshly ground black pepper, to taste

1 (1.25-ounce) envelope onion soup mix

4 tablespoons mayonnaise

1 tablespoon Dijon mustard

1 banana shallot, chopped

3/4 pound Gorgonzola cheese, crumbled

16 miniature burger buns

Directions

- Preheat a sous vide water bath to 145 degrees F.
- Thoroughly combine ground meat, salt, pepper, and envelope onion soup mix in a mixing dish.
- Shape the mixture into 16 meatballs with your hands. Flatten each portion into a small patty, about 1/2-inches-thick.
- Transfer the prepared patties to cooking pouches; seal tightly.
- Submerge the cooking pouches in the water bath; cook for 3 hours.
- Heat a grill pan over medium-high flame. Grill burgers for 1 to 2 minutes on each side, working in batches.
- Divide the mayonnaise, mustard and shallot among the bottom buns. Now, top each with a slider, and finish with Gorgonzola cheese. Cover with the top of the bun and serve immediately.

165. Perfect Lil Smokies
(Ready in about 2 hours | Servings 8)

This recipe is really as easy as it sounds. Be inspired by little cocktail sausages and make your parties memorable!
Per serving: 314 Calories; 20.4g Fat; 10.8g Carbs; 21.6g Protein; 3.5g Sugars

Ingredients

2 pounds cocktail sausages
1 (12-ounce) bottle chili sauce

Directions

- Preheat a sous vide water bath to 140 degrees F.
- Add cocktail sausages and chili sauce to cooking pouches; seal tightly.
- Submerge the cooking pouches in the water bath; cook for 2 hours.
- Serve with toothpicks and enjoy!

---

166. Mini Pork Carnitas
(Ready in about 18 hours 10 minutes | Servings 12)

Juicy pulled pork in elegant wonton wraps. This is such a brilliant idea! Undoubtedly, your guests will be impressed with the deliciousness of these bites.
Per serving: 405 Calories; 23.4g Fat; 14.4g Carbs; 32.4g Protein; 3.5g Sugars

Ingredients

3 pounds boneless pork butt
Sea salt and ground black pepper, to taste
2 garlic cloves, smashed
1 habanero pepper, deseeded and minced
1 cup ale
1/2 cup bone broth

1 teaspoon dried basil
1 teaspoon dried rosemary
2 bay leaves
24 wonton wraps
1 cup Queso Manchego, shredded
1 cup Pico de gallo, for garnish

Directions

- Preheat a sous vide water bath to 145 degrees F.
- Place pork, salt, pepper, garlic, habanero pepper, ale, bone broth, basil, rosemary, and bay leaves in cooking pouches; seal tightly.
- Submerge the cooking pouches in the water bath; cook for 18 hours. Remove sous vide pork from the cooking pouches and shred with two forks.
- Preheat your oven to 380 degrees F. Spritz a mini muffin pan with a nonstick cooking spray.
- Fill wonton wraps with shredded pork. Top with shredded Queso Manchego. Bake about 9 minutes.
- Remove from the oven; allow them to cool for 5 minutes before serving. Serve with Pico de gallo on the side. Bon appétit!

167. Italian-Style Tomato Dipping Sauce
(Ready in about 45 minutes | Servings 10)

Tomato is a powerhouse of vitamin K, vitamin A, vitamin C, vitamin B6, manganese, potassium, thiamine, and dietary fiber. Tomatoes can protect your heart, improve vision, and manage diabetes.

Per serving: 71 Calories; 4.3g Fat; 5.6g Carbs; 3.3g Protein; 3.4g Sugars

Ingredients

2 pounds very ripe tomatoes, chopped with juices

1 cup scallions, chopped

3 cloves roasted garlic, pressed

2 teaspoons dried Italian herb seasoning

2 heaping tablespoons fresh cilantro, roughly chopped

Sea salt and ground black pepper, to taste

1 teaspoon red pepper flakes

1 teaspoon sugar

2 tablespoons extra-virgin olive oil

1 cup Parmigiano-Reggiano cheese, preferably freshly grated

Directions

- Preheat a sous vide water bath to 180 degrees F.
- Add all ingredients, minus cheese, to cooking pouches; seal tightly.
- Submerge the cooking pouches in the water bath; cook for 40 minutes.
- Place the prepared sous vide sauce in a serving bowl; top with grated Parmigiano-Reggiano cheese and serve with breadsticks. Bon appétit!

---

168. Creamy and Cheesy Seafood Dip
(Ready in about 40 minutes | Servings 12)

This dipping sauce is definitely one of the best options to make you snack a delicious pleasure. Doubtless, it's easy to add plenty of seafood to your diet!

Per serving: 206 Calories; 10.2g Fat; 2.2g Carbs; 25g Protein; 0.2g Sugars

Ingredients

6 ounces scallops, chopped

6 ounces shrimp, chopped

2 cups broth, preferably homemade

1 ½ cups Colby cheese, shredded

1 ½ cups Gruyere cheese, shredded

1/2 teaspoon smoked paprika

1/2 teaspoons ground black pepper

1/2 teaspoon dried oregano

Directions

- Preheat a sous vide water bath to 132 degrees F.
- Simply put all ingredients into cooking pouches; seal tightly.
- Submerge the cooking pouches in the water bath; cook for 35 minutes.
- Transfer the sous vide dipping sauce to a nice serving bowl; serve with dippers of choice. Bon appétit!

VEGAN

169. Green Beans with Pine Nuts and Basil
(Ready in about 50 minutes | Servings 4)

Green beans can boost your immune system and improve your vision. Further, they can help you reduce the risk of cancer and heart diseases. Impressive!

Per serving: 197 Calories; 15.8g Fat; 13.3g Carbs; 4.7g Protein; 2.8g Sugars

Ingredients

1 ½ pounds green beans

1 medium-sized leek, sliced

2 cloves garlic, minced

1/2 teaspoon dried dill weed

1 tablespoon peanut oil

1/2 cup pine nuts, toasted

1/4 cup fresh basil, chopped

Directions

- Preheat a sous vide water bath to 183 degrees F.
- Place green beans, leek, garlic, dill, and peanut oil in cooking pouches; seal tightly.
- Submerge the cooking pouches in the water bath; cook for 45 minutes. Remove the sous vide green beans from the cooking pouches.
- Serve garnished with toasted pine nuts and fresh basil. Bon appétit!

---

170. Summer-Style Corn on the Cob
(Ready in about 30 minutes | Servings 6)

Corn on the cob with a tangy avocado and lime dressing. The flavors are fantastic!

Per serving: 187 Calories; 6.6g Fat; 31.9g Carbs; 6.2g Protein; 5.4g Sugars

Ingredients

6 ears of corn, ends trimmed

Sea salt and ground black pepper, to taste

1 tablespoon dried parsley flakes

1 avocado

1 clove garlic, minced

2 tablespoons fresh cilantro, minced

2 tablespoons fresh lemon juice

1 tablespoon nutritional yeast

1 teaspoon hot paprika

1 teaspoon red pepper flakes

Directions

- Preheat a sous vide water bath to 183 degrees F.
- Place corn, salt, pepper, and dried parsley flakes in cooking pouches; seal tightly.
- Submerge the cooking pouches in the water bath; cook for 25 minutes. Remove the sous vide corn from the cooking pouches.
- Meanwhile, mix avocado with garlic, fresh cilantro, lemon juice, nutritional yeast, and paprika; mix to combine well.
- Spread this avocado mixture on the corn; sprinkle with red pepper flakes and serve immediately. Bon appétit!

171. Asian-Style Vegetable Soup
(Ready in about 1 hour | Servings 4)

This recipe is so easy to prepare because there's no sautéing at all, so that the only real work is prepare your vegetables.
Per serving: 304 Calories; 20.4g Fat; 26.1g Carbs; 7.1g Protein; 8.9g Sugars

Ingredients

2 carrots, sliced

2 parsnips, sliced

1 celery with leaves, chopped

2 shallots, chopped

1 garlic clove, minced

2 cups Swiss chard

5 cups roasted vegetable broth

2 tablespoons sesame oil

1 teaspoon dried nori

1/2 teaspoon coriander

Salt and ground black pepper, to taste

1/4 cup white miso

1/4 cup chopped fresh cilantro leaves, for garnish

Directions

- Preheat a sous vide water bath to 183 degrees F.
- Place the vegetables, broth, sesame oil, dried nori, coriander, salt, and black pepper in cooking pouches; seal tightly.
- Submerge the cooking pouches in the water bath; cook for 60 minutes. Transfer the mixture to a bowl.
- Add miso paste to the bowl and stir to combine well.
- Now, puree the sous vide vegetables and cooking liquid with an immersion blender until silky and smooth.
- Ladle into individual bowls, garnish with fresh cilantro leaves and serve hot.

---

172. Nana's Spicy Mashed Potatoes
(Ready in about 1 hour 5 minutes | Servings 4)

Adding the onion and garlic is an easy way to flavor mashed potatoes, but sautéed onions and garlic will add much better deep taste.
Per serving: 275 Calories; 13.8g Fat; 35.3g Carbs; 4.3g Protein; 3.9g Sugars

Ingredients

1 ½ pounds potatoes, peeled and diced

4 tablespoons olive oil

Salt and black pepper, to taste

1 red onion, finely chopped

2 garlic cloves, minced

1 teaspoon chipotle pepper, minced

1 teaspoon cayenne pepper

1 tablespoon fresh parsley, roughly chopped

Directions

- Preheat a sous vide water bath to 185 degrees F.
- Place potatoes, 1 tablespoon of olive oil, salt, and black pepper in cooking pouches; seal tightly.
- Submerge the cooking pouches in the water bath; cook for 60 minutes. Remove the potatoes from the cooking pouches and pat them dry.
- Mash your potatoes and reserve.
- Then, heat the oil in a sauté pan that is preheated over a moderately high heat. Sweat the onion until softened and translucent.
- Add garlic and chipotle pepper; cook an additional 1 minute or until aromatic.
- Add cayenne pepper and mashed potatoes to the pan; stir to combine well. Serve garnished with fresh parsley. Enjoy!

173. Brussels Sprout and Cauliflower Curry
(Ready in about 1 hour | Servings 6)

Is there anything better than a rich, warm curry during autumn weekdays? Serve warm with rice, pasta, or crusty bread.
Per serving: 127 Calories; 5.5g Fat; 17.8g Carbs; 5.5g Protein; 6.7g Sugars

Ingredients

1 pound cauliflower, broken into florets

1 pound Brussels sprouts, halved

Sea salt and ground black pepper, to taste

1/2 teaspoon dried dill

1/2 teaspoon dried rosemary

1 bay leaf

2 tablespoons coconut oil

1 banana shallot, chopped

1 tablespoon fresh ginger root, minced

3 cloves garlic, smashed

2 tablespoons curry paste

2 tomatoes, chopped

1 (14-ounce) can coconut milk

1 tablespoon lime juice

Directions

- Preheat a sous vide water bath to 183 degrees F.
- Place cauliflower, Brussels sprouts, salt, black pepper, dill, rosemary, and bay leaf in cooking pouches; seal tightly.
- Submerge the cooking pouches in the water bath; cook for 45 minutes.
- Meanwhile, heat coconut oil a deep pan over a moderate flame. Now, sweat the shallot, ginger, and garlic for 2 to 3 minutes, stirring continuously.
- Add curry paste and continue to cook for 1 minute more. Now, add tomatoes and coconut milk. Turn the heat to medium-high and bring to a boil.
- Now, decrease the heat to low to maintain a simmer; simmer approximately 6 minutes to allow the flavors to develop.
- Afterwards, add lime juice, stir, and serve warm. Bon appétit!

---

174. Butternut Squash Soup with Tofu
(Ready in about 1 hour 15 minutes | Servings 6)

Butternut squash is an extremely healthy and flavorful addition to your vegan recipes. In this recipe, butternut squash is cooked with coconut oil and served with pan-fried tofu. A harmony of tastes!
Per serving: 173 Calories; 10.4g Fat; 17.8g Carbs; 5.9g Protein; 0.6g Sugars

Ingredients

2 pounds butternut squash, seeded, thinly sliced

Himalayan salt and white pepper, to taste

1 tablespoon coconut oil, room temperature

2 tablespoons grapeseed oil

1/2 pound extra-firm tofu, pressed and cut into cubes

1 teaspoon cayenne pepper

2 tablespoons fresh chives, roughly chopped

2 tablespoons roasted pepitas, for garnish

Directions

- Preheat a sous vide water bath to 183 degrees F.
- Add butternut squash, salt, white pepper, and coconut oil to cooking pouches; seal tightly.
- Submerge the cooking pouches in the water bath; cook for 60 minutes.
- Heat grapeseed oil in a pan over a moderate flame. Sauté tofu cubes for 10 minutes, stirring once, until they are evenly browned. Coat with cayenne pepper on all sides.
- Ladle warm butternut squash soup into individual bowls and top with pan-fried tofu cubes. Garnish with chives and roasted pepitas. Enjoy!

175. Tangy Braised Cabbage
(Ready in about 1 hour 5 minutes | Servings 4)

A soft and tangy cabbage that is seasoned and cooked sous vide. Just like grandma used to make!
Per serving: 122 Calories; 7.1g Fat; 16.9g Carbs; 2.2g Protein; 7.8g Sugars

Ingredients

1 large-sized head green cabbage, cored, torn into pieces
1/4 cup balsamic vinegar
Salt and freshly ground black pepper
1 teaspoon smoked cayenne pepper
2 tablespoons grapeseed oil

2 garlic cloves, minced
1 teaspoon dried basil
1/2 teaspoon dried oregano
1/2 teaspoon dried dill weed

Directions

- Preheat a sous vide water bath to 183 degrees F.
- Add the cabbage, vinegar, salt, black pepper, and cayenne pepper to cooking pouches; seal tightly.
- Submerge the cooking pouches in the water bath; cook for 60 minutes.
- After that, heat the oil in a saucepan over a moderately high heat. Once hot, fry the garlic along with dried basil, oregano, and dill weed for 1 minute or until aromatic.
- Add sous vide cabbage and continue to cook for a couple of minutes more or until everything is heated through. Serve immediately. Bon appétit!

---

176. Caramelized Onion Soup
(Ready in about 2 hours 25 minutes | Servings 4)

Yellow onions are carefully selected and magically transformed into a hearty French-style soup that is healthy as well. In this recipe, you can experiment and substitute the brown onion or sweet onion for yellow onion.
Per serving: 234 Calories; 9g Fat; 31.9g Carbs; 8.7g Protein; 17.7g Sugars

Ingredients

2 tablespoons olive oil
3 pounds yellow onions, sliced
Sea salt and ground white pepper, to taste
2 tablespoons dry white wine

2 cloves garlic, smashed
4 cups vegetable stock, preferably homemade
2 heaping tablespoons fresh cilantro, chopped

Directions

- Heat the olive oil in a cast-iron pan over medium-high heat. Now, sweat the onions with salt and white pepper until they're caramelized.
- Pour in white wine in order to scrape off any brown bits from the bottom of the pan.
- Preheat a sous vide water bath to 185 degrees F.
- Add the onion mixture and garlic to cooking pouches; seal tightly. Submerge the cooking pouches in the water bath; cook for 2 hours.
- Pour the contents of the cooking pouches to a large stockpot; add vegetable stock and bring to a rolling boil.
- Now, turn the heat to simmer; let it simmer, partially covered, for 20 minutes or until thoroughly heated.
- Ladle your soup into four bowls. Top with croutons or saltines of choice. Serve garnished with cilantro. Enjoy!

177. Easy and Tangy Swiss Chard
(Ready in about 1 hour 20 minutes | Servings 4)

A sautéed Swiss chard is an ultimate side dish and it goes with almost everything. You can cook a big batch and use for a couple of days with your favorite main dishes.

Per serving: 261 Calories; 27.4g Fat; 5.4g Carbs; 2.1g Protein; 1.9g Sugars

Ingredients

2 large bunches Swiss chard, torn into pieces

Kosher salt and black pepper, to taste

1 teaspoon crushed red pepper flakes

1/2 cup vegetable stock

1/2 cup scallions, chopped

2 tablespoons fresh lemon juice

Directions

- Preheat a sous vide water bath to 185 degrees F.
- Add all ingredients, except for lemon juice, to cooking pouches; seal tightly. Submerge the cooking pouches in the water bath; cook for 1 hour 15 minutes.
- Transfer the contents of the cooking pouches to a serving bowl.
- Drizzle fresh lemon juice over cooked chard and serve immediately. Bon appétit!

---

178. Artichoke Pasta Salad
(Ready in about 1 hour 15 minutes | Servings 4)

Artichokes are an excellent source of antioxidants and heart-healthy components. They can protect your liver and improve bone health too.

Per serving: 435 Calories; 25.9g Fat; 44.9g Carbs; 8.7g Protein; 5.1g Sugars

Ingredients

4 cups artichoke, trimmed

1 teaspoon kosher salt

1/2 teaspoon ground black pepper

1 (16-ounce) box short pasta

1 pint cherry tomatoes, halved

2 cucumbers, sliced

2 bell peppers, chopped

1 zucchini, thinly sliced

1 yellow onion, sliced thin

1/2 cup Kalamata olives, pitted and drained

1/4 cup extra virgin olive oil

1/4 cup champagne vinegar

1 teaspoon red pepper flakes, crushed

1/4 cup fresh basil, finely chopped

Directions

- Preheat a sous vide water bath to 183 degrees F.
- Add the artichokes, salt, and black pepper to cooking pouches; seal tightly. Submerge the cooking pouches in the water bath; cook for 1 hour 10 minutes.
- Remove the artichokes from the cooking pouches and allow them to cool completely.
- Now, cook pasta according to package instructions; drain, rinse and reserve.
- In a salad bowl, toss the artichokes, cold pasta, cherry tomatoes, cucumber, peppers, zucchini, onion, and Kalamata olives.
- In a small mixing bowl, whisk olive oil, vinegar and red pepper flakes. Dress the salad and serve garnished with fresh basil. Bon appétit!

179. Broccoli and Cauliflower Salad with Tahini Dressing
(Ready in about 35 minutes + chilling time | Servings 4)

A decadent tahini i.e. sesame paste will add a little something special to this salad. It's easy to prepare a home-style tahini by using sesame seeds and a good food processor.

Per serving: 199 Calories; 12.1g Fat; 14.1g Carbs; 14.4g Protein; 3.1g Sugars

Ingredients

1 head broccoli, cut into florets
1 head cauliflower, cut into florets
Coarse sea salt, to taste
1 teaspoon black peppercorns
2 tomatoes, sliced
1 red onion, thinly sliced

1/2 teaspoon oregano
1/2 teaspoon basil
1 tablespoon lemon juice, freshly squeezed
3 tablespoons tahini
1/2 cup mozzarella-style vegan cheese, crumbled

Directions

- Preheat a sous vide water bath to 183 degrees F.
- Season broccoli and cauliflower with salt.
- Add broccoli and cauliflower to cooking pouches; add black peppercorns to the pouches and seal tightly. Submerge the cooking pouches in the water bath; cook for 30 minutes.
- Remove the broccoli and cauliflower from the cooking pouches; pat dry your vegetables with kitchen towels and allow them to cool completely.
- Toss broccoli and cauliflower with tomatoes, onion, oregano, and basil.
- In a small dish, whisk the lemon juice and tahini until smooth. Drizzle over the salad and serve topped with mozzarella-style vegan cheese. Enjoy!

---

180. Delicious Overnight Oatmeal
(Ready in about 8 hours | Servings 4)

Never underestimate a power of overnight oatmeal. It is healthy, hearty and weight loss friendly.

Per serving: 184 Calories; 3.4g Fat; 48.8g Carbs; 8.3g Protein; 16.7g Sugars

Ingredients

2 cups rolled oats
6 cups water
Kosher salt, to taste
1/8 teaspoon freshly grated nutmeg
1/2 teaspoon whole star anise

Fruit Compote:
1/2 cup dried cranberries
1/2 cup dried sultanas
1/3 cup walnuts, chopped
1/4 cup brown sugar
1 cup water
1 stick cinnamon
1/2 teaspoon coconut extract
1 teaspoon vanilla extract
1 teaspoon lemon zest

Directions

- Preheat a sous vide water bath to 150 degrees F.
- Place the oats, 6 cups of water, salt, nutmeg, and star anise in the cooking pouch; seal tightly.
- In another cooking pouch, place the fruits, walnuts, sugar, a cup of water, cinnamon, coconut extract, vanilla extract, and lemon zest.
- Submerge the cooking pouches in the water bath; cook for 8 hours or overnight.
- On an actual day, divide the oatmeal between serving bowls; top each serving with fruit compote and enjoy!

181. Easy Bhindi Masala
(Ready in about 30 minutes | Servings 4)

Reshampatti is a type of hot Indian chili powder. Feel free to use any other type of chili powder you can have on hand.
Per serving: 115 Calories; 7.1g Fat; 12.4g Carbs; 2.7g Protein; 3.7g Sugars

Ingredients

1 pound fresh okra pods, washed and trimmed

1 teaspoon garlic paste

Seasoned salt and white pepper, to taste

2 tablespoons olive oil

1/2 teaspoon brown mustard seeds

6 fresh curry leaves

1 brown onion, chopped

1/2 teaspoon cayenne pepper

1/4 teaspoon reshampatti

Directions

- Preheat a sous vide water bath to 176 degrees F.
- Simply put the okra into a large-sized cooking pouch. Then, add garlic paste, salt and white pepper to the pouch; seal tightly.
- Submerge the cooking pouch in the water bath; cook for 20 minutes.
- Now, heat 1 teaspoon of the oil in a wok or sauté pan over a moderately high heat. Cook brown mustard seeds and curry leaves until aromatic, stirring constantly.
- Heat another tablespoon of the oil. Stir in the onion; sweat the onion until tender and translucent. Transfer the contents of the cooking pouch to the pan.
- Add cayenne pepper and reshampatti and cook an additional 3 to 4 minutes or until everything is heated through. Serve warm and enjoy!

---

182. Zucchini with Sun-Dried Tomato Pesto
(Ready in about 45 minutes | Servings 4)

Turn a humble zucchini into a delicious and sophisticated family meal. Each ingredient in this light and refreshing dish plays a part in its rich and incredible flavor.
Per serving: 175 Calories; 10.1g Fat; 14.9g Carbs; 11.5g Protein; 2.7g Sugars

Ingredients

2 pounds zucchini, cut into thick slices

1 ½ cups fresh basil, packed

1/4 cup pine nuts

2 large-sized cloves garlic, peeled

3 teaspoons lemon juice

3 tablespoons nutritional yeast

Salt and pepper, to taste

1/4 cup sun-dried tomatoes, chopped

2 tablespoons extra-virgin olive oil

4-5 tablespoons water

Directions

- Preheat a sous vide water bath to 183 degrees F.
- Place zucchini in cooking pouches; seal tightly.
- Submerge the cooking pouches in the water bath; cook for 40 minutes. You can grill zucchinis on a grill pan if desired.
- Add basil, pine nuts, garlic, lemon juice, nutritional yeast, salt, pepper, and sun-dried tomatoes to your food processor or a high-powered blender; mix until a paste consistency forms.
- Slowly and gradually pour in the olive oil and continue mixing; add a few tablespoons of water to achieve your desired consistency.
- Serve the prepared zucchini with vegan pesto on the side. Bon appétit!

183. Luxurious Mushroom and Walnut Pâté
(Ready in about 1 hour | Servings 10)

Mushrooms are easy to cook sous vide. In addition to the tasty flavor, this pâté has a lot of amazing and delicate textures. Serve with a home-made cornbread.

Per serving: 73 Calories; 6.8g Fat; 2.2g Carbs; 1.8g Protein; 1.1g Sugars

Ingredients

1 pound Cremini mushrooms
Salt and freshly ground black pepper
1 teaspoon red pepper flakes
4 tablespoons olive oil
2 sprigs rosemary

2 sprigs thyme
1/2 cup green onions, chopped
2 cloves garlic, chopped
1/4 cup toasted walnuts

Directions

- Preheat a sous vide water bath to 183 degrees F.
- Then, place mushrooms, salt, black pepper, red pepper flakes, 2 tablespoons of olive oil, rosemary, and thyme to cooking pouches; seal tightly.
- Submerge the cooking pouches in the water bath; cook for 50 minutes. Remove the mushrooms from the cooking pouches.
- Then, in the preheated skillet, cook green onions and garlic until just softened and fragrant. Allow this sautéed mixture to cool to room temperature.
- In your food processor, process the walnuts until a butter-like consistency is achieved. Add sautéed mixture and sous vide mushrooms.
- Process until creamy and smooth. Place in your refrigerator until ready to serve. Bon appétit!

---

184. Sweet Potato Purée
(Ready in about 1 hour | Servings 4)

You don't have to be a vegan to enjoy this belly-warming dish. It's so packed with perfectly cooked sweet potatoes, vegan cream and spices that you won't miss butter or milk.

Per serving: 144 Calories; 7.4g Fat; 18.2g Carbs; 5g Protein; 1.8g Sugars

Ingredients

1 ½ pounds sweet potatoes, diced
Sea salt, to taste
1/4 teaspoon ground black pepper, to taste
10 ounces canned coconut milk

2 tablespoons vegan sour cream
2 tablespoons vegan butter
1 teaspoon curry
1/2 teaspoon cayenne pepper

Directions

- Preheat a sous vide water bath to 183 degrees F.
- Add sweet potatoes to cooking pouches; seal tightly.
- Submerge the cooking pouches in the water bath; cook for 60 minutes.
- Now, mash the sweet potatoes to the desired consistency; add the remaining ingredients and mix until everything is well incorporated. Bon appétit!

185. Zingy Summer Chickpea Salad
(Ready in about 3 hours + chilling time | Servings 6)

Chickpea is one of the most incredible staples of a vegan diet. By cooking them in pouches, you help retain a unique texture and delicate flavor.

Per serving: 266 Calories; 12.5g Fat; 31.5g Carbs; 9.5g Protein; 6.4g Sugars

Ingredients

1/2 pound dried chickpeas
4 cups water
1/2 cup scallions, chopped
1 avocado, peeled, pitted, diced
2 red bell peppers, thinly sliced
2 green bell peppers, thinly sliced
4 tomatoes, sliced
3 cucumbers, sliced
1/2 cup Kalamata olives, pitted and halved
1/4 cup fresh parsley leaves, roughly chopped

Dressing:
1/4 cup champagne vinegar
1 tablespoon Dijon mustard
1/4 cup extra-virgin olive oil
1 teaspoon red pepper flakes, crushed
Sea salt, to taste
1/4 teaspoon black pepper, preferably freshly ground

Directions

- Soak chickpeas in water overnight; drain and rinse.
- Preheat a sous vide water bath to 195 degrees F.
- Add chickpeas and water to cooking pouches; seal tightly.
- Submerge the cooking pouches in the water bath; cook for 3 hours. Remove chickpeas from the cooking pouches and allow them to cool completely.
- Add the chickpeas to a large salad bowl. Add the scallions, avocado, peppers, tomatoes, cucumber, and olives.
- In a mixing dish, whisk the vinegar with Dijon mustard, olive oil, red pepper, salt, and black pepper.
- Dress your salad and toss to combine. Garnish with fresh parsley and serve well-chilled. Enjoy!

186. Easy Creamy Corn Chowder
(Ready in about 35 minutes | Servings 4)

This recipe uses the sous vide technique for cooking corn so you get a soup full of balanced flavors and rich textures.

Per serving: 316 Calories; 20.7g Fat; 33.1g Carbs; 9.7g Protein; 9.6g Sugars

Ingredients

3 ears corn, kernels sliced off
2 tablespoons olive oil
Sea salt, to taste
1/2 teaspoon ground black pepper
2 tablespoons cilantro, chopped

2 tablespoons scallions, chopped
2 Cascabel chilies, chopped
3 cups vegetable broth
1 cup rice milk, unsweetened
1 cup smoky paprika croutons

Directions

- Preheat a sous vide water bath to 183 degrees F.
- Add corn, olive oil, salt, black pepper, cilantro, scallions, chilies, and vegetable broth to cooking pouches; seal tightly.
- Submerge the cooking pouches in the water bath; cook for 25 minutes. Transfer the contents of the cooking pouches to a stockpot.
- Add unsweetened rice milk and bring to a simmer; let it simmer for 5 to 6 minutes or until the soup is heated through.
- Ladle the soup into serving bowls and serve garnished with paprika croutons. Bon appétit!

187. Savory Oatmeal with Mushrooms
(Ready in about 4 hours 10 minutes | Servings 4)

In this hearty, savory dish, oatmeal is topped with sautéed mushrooms and baby spinach. This is one of the best and most fulfilling breakfasts for the whole family.

Per serving: 297 Calories; 9g Fat; 60.9g Carbs; 9.9g Protein; 2.2g Sugars

Ingredients

1 cup steel-cut oats

4 cups water

1/2 teaspoon sea salt

1/2 teaspoon ground black pepper

1/2 teaspoon cayenne pepper

2 tablespoons grapeseed oil

8 ounces brown mushrooms, sliced

1/2 medium onion, chopped

4 cloves garlic, minced

3 sprigs fresh thyme

1 cup baby spinach

Directions

- Preheat a sous vide water bath to 175 degrees F.
- Place steel-cut oats, water, salt, black pepper, and cayenne pepper in cooking pouches; seal tightly.
- Submerge the cooking pouches in the water bath; cook for 4 hours; reserve.
- Heat the oil in a pan that is preheated over a moderately high heat. Sauté the mushrooms, onion, and garlic until softened.
- Now, add fresh thyme and continue cooking an additional 5 minutes. Spoon mushroom mixture over the prepared oatmeal. Top with baby spinach and serve warm. Bon appétit!

---

188. Spicy Kidney Beans
(Ready in about 6 hours 35 minutes | Servings 3)

Did you know that dried beans don't require an overnight soak? Cook them sous vide and see the difference.

Per serving: 255 Calories; 9.8g Fat; 33.6g Carbs; 10.4g Protein; 6.5g Sugars

Ingredients

2 cups dried red kidney beans

3 cloves garlic, crushed

2 bay leaves

1/2 teaspoon black peppercorns

1 teaspoon cayenne pepper

Sea salt, to taste

5 cups water

2 tablespoons olive oil

1 yellow onion, peeled and chopped

2 celery stalks, finely diced

2 bell peppers, finely diced

1/2 teaspoon chili flakes

Directions

- Preheat a sous vide water bath to 194 degrees F.
- Place red kidney beans, garlic, bay leaves, black peppercorns, cayenne pepper, salt, and water in cooking pouches; seal tightly.
- Submerge the cooking pouches in the water bath; cook for 6 hours 30 minutes. Remove the beans form the cooking pouches, reserving the cooking liquid.
- Heat olive oil in a pan that is preheated over a moderate heat. Once hot, sauté the onions, celery and peppers until they are softened.
- Add the cooking liquid to deglaze the bottom of your pan. Add reserved beans and chili flakes and cook an additional 5 minutes or until heated through. Bon appétit!

189. Delicious Lentil Curry
(Ready in about 1 hour 40 minutes | Servings 4)

Lentils are an excellent source of vitamin B1, dietary fiber, phosphorous, manganese, iron, and so on. It can help you control diabetes, improve heart health and digestion.
Per serving: 274 Calories; 21.7g Fat; 19.6g Carbs; 5.8g Protein; 4.5g Sugars

Ingredients

2 tablespoons grapeseed oil
1 cup leeks, chopped
2 parsnips, chopped
2 carrots, chopped
2 stalks celery, chopped
2 cloves garlic, crushed
Sea salt, to taste
1/3 teaspoon freshly ground black pepper
3 cups water

2 cups yellow lentils
2 sprigs fresh rosemary
2 sprigs fresh thyme
2 bay leaves
1 tablespoon curry powder
1 teaspoon garam masala
1/2 teaspoon fresh ginger, ground
1 cup full-fat coconut milk

Directions

- Preheat a sous vide water bath to 183 degrees F.
- Heat the oil in a pan over moderate heat. Once hot, sauté the leeks, parsnip, carrots, celery, and garlic for 4 minutes.
- Add the salt and black pepper. Place this sautéed mixture in cooking pouches; add the water, lentils, rosemary, thyme, and bay leaves to the pouches; seal tightly.
- Submerge the cooking pouches in the water bath; cook for 1 hour 30 minutes.
- Transfer the contents of the cooking pouches to a large stockpot; add the remaining ingredients and let it simmer an additional 10 minutes or until thoroughly heated.
- Ladle into individual bowls and serve warm. Bon appétit!

---

190. Fried Tofu in Peanut Sauce
(Ready in about 1 hour 40 minutes | Servings 3)

This recipe cooks tofu in peanut oil and spice mixture, which results in the most delicious tofu ever!
Per serving: 235 Calories; 16.5g Fat; 8.7g Carbs; 16.7g Protein; 4.4g Sugars

Ingredients

16 ounces firm tofu, drained and sliced
1 tablespoon peanut oil
2 cloves garlic, roughly minced
Celery salt and freshly ground black pepper, to taste
1 teaspoon curry powder

Peanut Sauce:
2 tablespoons peanut butter
4 tablespoons soymilk
1 tablespoon soy sauce
1/2 teaspoon chili powder
1/2 teaspoon mustard seeds
1/2 teaspoon celery seeds
Salt, to taste

Directions

- Preheat a sous vide water bath to 183 degrees F.
- Add tofu, 1 tablespoon of peanut oil, garlic, salt, black pepper, and curry powder to cooking pouches; seal tightly.
- Submerge the cooking pouches in the water bath; cook for 1 hour 30 minutes; reserve cooking liquids.
- Heat a cast-iron pan over a moderately high heat; fry tofu slices for 3 to 4 minutes or until they are lightly browned on both sides.
- In a saucepan, simmer peanut butter, soy milk, soy sauce, chili powder, mustard seeds, and celery seeds for 2 to 3 minutes.
- Add the reserved tofu and sprinkle with salt to taste. Serve warm. Bon appétit!

191. Skinny Mediterranean-Style Quinoa
(Ready in about 1 hour | Servings 4)

Quinoa is one of the healthiest foods on the planet. It is a powerful source of vegan protein, iron, dietary fiber, antioxidants, and so on. Quinoa is nicely adaptable to any flavor combination you like.

Per serving: 330 Calories; 11.7g Fat; 47.2g Carbs; 10.1g Protein; 2.8g Sugars

Ingredients

1 ½ cups quinoa, rinsed

1 teaspoon dried oregano

1 teaspoon dried basil

1 teaspoon garlic, minced

1/2 teaspoon fresh ginger, grated

Kosher salt, to taste

1/4 teaspoon ground black pepper

A pinch of freshly grated nutmeg

2 ½ cups water

2 tablespoons olive oil

2 zucchinis, sliced

1 red onion, peeled and chopped

2 tomatoes, chopped

1/4 cup black olives, pitted and sliced

Directions

- Preheat a sous vide water bath to 183 degrees F.
- Place the quinoa, oregano, basil, garlic, ginger, salt, black pepper, nutmeg, and water in cooking pouches; seal tightly.
- Submerge the cooking pouches in the water bath; cook for 50 minutes; drain and fluff the quinoa.
- In a sauté pan, heat olive oil over medium-high heat; now, sauté zucchinis and onion until tender.
- Stir in tomatoes and cook an additional 5 minutes, stirring periodically. Stir in reserved quinoa and serve garnished with black olives. Bon appétit!

DESSERTS

192. Chocolate and Bananas Bars with Walnuts
(Ready in about 40 minutes + freezing time | Servings 6)

This dessert makes itself. You can also customize the flavor by adding mint, coconut, hazelnuts, or dried cranberries.
Per serving: 277 Calories; 18.8g Fat; 26.5g Carbs; 3g Protein; 13.9g Sugars

Ingredients

1 pound bananas, peeled and sliced
1/4 cup walnut butter
4 ounces semi-sweet chocolate chunks

1/3 cup walnuts, chopped
A pinch of grated nutmeg

Directions

- Preheat a sous vide water bath to 138 degrees F.
- Simply put all of the above ingredients, except for walnuts, in a cooking pouch; seal tightly.
- Submerge the cooking pouch in the water bath; cook for 35 minutes.
- Pour the chocolate mixture into candy molds. Now, scatter chopped walnuts over the top and freeze until solid. Enjoy!

---

193. Refreshing Orange Pudding
(Ready in about 45 minutes | Servings 5)

Try a refreshing, citrusy pudding in ramekins. Sous vide works wonders with easy-to-find ingredients and makes the best desserts you can imagine.
Per serving: 175 Calories; 7.2g Fat; 19.7g Carbs; 7.1g Protein; 12.5g Sugars

Ingredients

1/2 teaspoon coconut oil, melted
3 eggs
1/2 cup milk
1/3 cup freshly squeezed orange juice

6 tablespoons granulated sugar
1 teaspoon vanilla essence
1/2 teaspoon ground star anise
1/3 cup fine white flour

Directions

- Brush each ramekin with a melted coconut oil.
- Mix the egg yolks, milk, orange juice, sugar, vanilla, star anise, and flour with a whisk; beat until everything is well mixed.
- In the meantime, cream the egg whites with an electric mixer.
- Now, fold the eggs whites into the yolk mixture; gently stir to combine.
- Spoon the mixture into 5 ramekins. Preheat a sous vide water bath to 180 degrees F.
- Place the ramekins on the baking rack in the preheated water bath and cover with a piece of aluminum foil; cook for 40 minutes.
- Remove ramekins from the water bath with a jar lifter or tongs. Serve topped with whipped cream if desired. Bon appétit!

194. Crème Caramel Croissant Pudding
(Ready in about 1 hour 35 minutes | Servings 6)

This is not a regular caramel bread pudding. This is a sous vide croissant pudding! This recipe has a rich and layered texture thanks to double cream, croissant, bourbon, and dried cherries. Here is a trick to steal from pro chefs – soak dried cherries in bourbon 15 minutes in advance.

Per serving: 451 Calories; 30.7g Fat; 33.9g Carbs; 10.8g Protein; 23.7g Sugars

Ingredients

1 ¼ cups double cream
3/4 cup milk
1 teaspoon vanilla paste
A pinch of table salt
1/4 teaspoon nutmeg, preferably freshly grated
4 eggs, lightly whisked

2 tablespoons bourbon
1/4 cup brown sugar
1/4 cup honey
1/4 cup butter, melted
6 stale croissants, torn into pieces
1/3 cup dried cherries

Directions

- Preheat a sous vide water bath to 175 degrees F.
- In a mixing dish, thoroughly combine double cream, milk, vanilla, salt, nutmeg, eggs, bourbon, sugar, honey and butter. Fold in the croissants and dried cherries; gently stir to combine well.
- Spoon this mixture into 12 lightly-greased ramekins. Place ramekins in a baking dish and then, place the baking dish in a large-sized cooking pouch; seal tightly.
- Place the ramekins on the baking rack; cook for 1 hour 30 minutes.
- Place ramekins under preheated broiler until they are golden brown on top or about 3 minutes. Serve and enjoy!

---

195. Jasmine Rice Pudding with Walnuts
(Ready in about 3 hours 35 minutes | Servings 4)

Your family will gobble up this aromatic dessert! Serve with some extra walnuts if desired. Toasted walnuts will add special charm to this rice pudding.

Per serving: 461 Calories; 16.1g Fat; 80.5g Carbs; 11g Protein; 60.5g Sugars

Ingredients

1 cup jasmine rice
3 cups whole milk
3 cups water
1 cup brown sugar
1/3 cup walnuts, ground
1/2 cup golden raisins

1/2 teaspoon ground cardamom
1/2 teaspoon ground cinnamon
1/4 teaspoon grated nutmeg
1/2 teaspoon vanilla essence
1/4 teaspoon salt

Directions

- Preheat a sous vide water bath to 183 degrees F.
- Simply put all ingredients into a cooking pouch; seal tightly.
- Submerge the cooking pouch in the water bath; cook for 3 hours 30 minutes.
- Serve warm or cold. Bon appétit!

196. Old Fashioned Chocolate Custard
(Ready in about 35 minutes | Servings 4)

Eggs are a key ingredient and crucial part of a traditional homemade custard. There is a reason that old-fashioned recipes call for eggs every time.

Per serving: 306 Calories; 18.9g Fat; 30.3g Carbs; 7.5g Protein; 24.4g Sugars

Ingredients

4 egg yolks
3/4 cup granulated sugar
1 cup milk
1 cup double cream
1 teaspoon vanilla bean paste
1/4 teaspoon ground cinnamon

1/4 teaspoon ground star anise
A pinch of salt
A pinch of ground cardamom
4 tablespoons cocoa powder
1 tablespoon corn flour

Directions

- Preheat a sous vide water bath to 150 degrees F.
- Beat egg yolks and granulated sugar with an electric mixer until creamy and very thick.
- With the mixer running, add the milk, double cream, vanilla, cinnamon, star anise, salt, cardamom, cocoa powder, and corn flour.
- Now, continue to blend until everything is well incorporated.
- Place the mixture in a cooking pouch; seal tightly. Submerge the cooking pouch in the water bath; cook for 30 minutes.
- Chill in an ice bath until cold. Place in your refrigerator overnight and serve well-chilled. Bon appétit!

197. Vanilla Ice Cream with Summer Compote
(Ready in about 1 hour | Servings 6)

Here's the perfect summer dessert. Who can say no to a vanilla ice cream with fruits? These stewed fruits are a great addition to your waffles, pancakes, and oatmeal too.

Per serving: 325 Calories; 14.8g Fat; 47.3g Carbs; 5.1g Protein; 37.9g Sugars

Ingredients

1/2 pound apricots
1/2 pound peaches
1/4 cup sugar
2 tablespoons raw honey
2 vanilla beans

1 cinnamon stick
1 teaspoon whole cloves
1/4 teaspoon ginger, freshly grated
3 tablespoons fresh orange juice
1 ½ pints vanilla ice cream

Directions

- Preheat a sous vide water bath to 183 degrees F.
- Simply put all ingredients, except for vanilla ice cream, into a cooking pouch; seal tightly.
- Submerge the cooking pouch in the water bath; cook for 1 hour. Remove the fruits from the cooking pouch.
- Serve with vanilla ice cream and enjoy!

198. Poached Apples with Orange Syrup
(Ready in about 3 hours | Servings 4)

A perfect afternoon snack, this dessert recipe can be doubled easily and prepared a few days in advance. Serve with whipped cream if desired.
Per serving: 252 Calories; 11.8g Fat; 39.2g Carbs; 0.7g Protein; 31.9g Sugars

Ingredients

4 Pink Lady apples, cored
4 tablespoons butter, melted
4 tablespoons powdered sugar

Orange Syrup:
1 tablespoon water
2 tablespoons powdered sugar
1/4 cup orange juice
1/2 teaspoon cornstarch mixed with 1/4 teaspoon cold water

Directions

- Preheat a sous vide water bath to 185 degrees F.
- Brush the apples with melted butter. Add the apples to cooking pouches. Now, add 4 tablespoons of powdered sugar and toss to coat apples on all sides; seal tightly.
- Submerge the cooking pouch in the water bath; cook for 3 hours.
- Meanwhile, make the syrup. In a saucepan that is preheated over high heat, cook the water and 2 tablespoons of powdered sugar until the sugar is completely dissolved.
- Now, pour in fresh orange juice and stir; reduce the heat to medium-high and stir for a couple of minutes.
- Add the cornstarch mixture to the saucepan and continue to cook, stirring frequently, until syrupy.
- Spoon the syrup over the stewed apples and serve. Bon appétit!

---

199. Poached Pears with Peanut Butter Sauce
(Ready in about 1 hour | Servings 6)

What is the most delicious way to get your daily serving of fruit? Make a fruit dessert! Pears filled with peanut butter sauce are way better than regular poached pears.
Per serving: 264 Calories; 7.6g Fat; 46.9g Carbs; 4.4g Protein; 41.5g Sugars

Ingredients

6 pears, peeled, cored and halved
1 ½ cups powdered sugar
1 teaspoon vanilla paste
1/2 cup Port wine

1/2 cup peanut butter
1/3 cup caramel flavored topping
1/2 cup warm water
3 tablespoons roasted peanuts, chopped

Directions

- Preheat a sous vide water bath to 183 degrees F.
- Add pears, powdered sugar, vanilla paste, and wine to cooking pouches; seal tightly.
- Submerge the cooking pouches in the water bath; cook for 50 minutes.
- Thoroughly combine peanut butter, caramel topping, and water until smooth; allow it to stand for 15 minutes.
- Arrange warm pears, cut side up, in individual serving bowls. Top each serving with peanut butter sauce.
- Sprinkle with chopped peanuts and serve. Bon appétit!

200. Dad's Plum Compote
(Ready in about 25 minutes | Servings 4)

Plums are an excellent source of vitamins, minerals, and dietary fiber. They contain powerful antioxidants as well. Serve this compote over ice cream, frozen yogurt, custard, waffles, and so forth.

Per serving: 92 Calories; 0.2g Fat; 23.3g Carbs; 0.6g Protein; 21.4g Sugars

Ingredients

12 ounces plums, halved and pitted
1 cup warm water
1 tablespoons lemon peel
2 tablespoons fresh orange juice
1/2 cup brown sugar

2 cinnamon sticks
3-4 whole star anise
3-4 whole cloves
1 vanilla bean

Directions

- Preheat a sous vide water bath to 167 degrees F.
- Place all the ingredients in cooking pouches; seal tightly.
- Submerge the cooking pouches in the water bath; cook for 20 minutes. Remove the plums from the cooking pouches.
- You can thicken the syrup in a saucepan. Allow your compote to cool slightly before serving. Bon appétit!

---

201. Bourbon Apple Butter
(Ready in about 1 hour 45 minutes | Servings 10)

This apple butter is cooked sous vide in a bourbon and spice mixture to develop deep flavors and rich texture.

Per serving: 109 Calories; 0.2g Fat; 25.7g Carbs; 0.3g Protein; 20.9g Sugars

Ingredients

6 apples, peeled, cored and diced
1/2 cup bourbon
1 cup water
2 teaspoons freshly squeezed lemon juice

2 cinnamon sticks
1 teaspoon whole cloves
1/2 cup maple syrup
1 vanilla bean

Directions

- Preheat a sous vide water bath to 185 degrees F.
- Place all of the above ingredients in cooking pouches; seal tightly.
- Submerge the cooking pouches in the water bath; cook for 1 hour 40 minutes.
- Store 2 weeks in the refrigerator or 6 months in the freezer. Enjoy!

202. Chocolate Raspberries Truffles
(Ready in about 3 hours 5 minutes + chilling time | Servings 10)

A rich and creamy mixture of a heavenly bittersweet chocolate, raspberries, heavy cream, and macadamia nuts. Is there a better way to satisfy your chocolate cravings?

Per serving: 259 Calories; 11.1g Fat; 40.7g Carbs; 2.6g Protein; 30g Sugars

Ingredients

1 pound bittersweet chocolate, chopped

1 cup fresh raspberries

1 ½ cups heavy cream

1/2 cup cocoa powder, unsweetened

1/3 cup macadamia nuts, chopped

2 tablespoons sugar

1/2 teaspoon cinnamon powder

1/2 teaspoon vanilla extract

Directions

- Preheat a sous vide water bath to 183 degrees F.
- Add all of the above ingredients to cooking pouches; seal tightly.
- Submerge the cooking pouches in the water bath; cook for 3 hours.
- Then, strain the mixture through a sieve; allow it to cool down to room temperature. Shape the mixture into balls.
- Afterwards, roll your balls in sprinkles or cocoa powder. Let them stand in the refrigerator until the chocolate is firm. Store in an airtight container. Bon appétit!

---

203. Autumn Crème Brûlée
(Ready in about 1 hour 30 minutes + chilling time | Servings 6)

Inspired by autumn, you can come up with a decadent and delicious crème brûlée. Finish your crème brûlée with a perfectly caramelized topping.

Per serving: 299 Calories; 25.5g Fat; 11g Carbs; 7.8g Protein; 8.7g Sugars

Ingredients

1 teaspoon coconut oil, melted

2 cups double cream

1/2 teaspoon ground cinnamon

1/4 teaspoon ground cardamom

1/4 teaspoon grated nutmeg

6 egg yolks

3 tablespoons red wine

2 teaspoons ginger syrup

1/2 cup pumpkin puree

1 teaspoon vanilla extract

1/3 cup granulated sugar

1/8 teaspoon kosher salt

Directions

- Preheat a sous vide water bath to 183 degrees F. Now, add a grill plate to the water bath. Grease 6 ramekins with melted coconut oil.
- Fill sous vide water bath with enough water to come within 1/4-inch of the top of your ramekins.
- In a pan, heat double cream, cinnamon, cardamom, and nutmeg over medium-low heat about 8 minutes.
- In the meantime, beat egg yolks, red wine, ginger syrup, pumpkin puree, vanilla extract, sugar, and salt with an electric mixer.
- Then, gradually fold in the cream/spice mixture into the egg/pumpkin mixture; mix until everything is well incorporated.
- Spoon the mixture into prepared ramekins and cover with aluminum foil.
- Lower the ramekins onto the prepared grill plate; cook for 1 hour 20 minutes. Place in the refrigerator for at least 3 hours.
- Afterwards, caramelize each serving under a broiler and serve.

OTHER SOUS VIDE FAVORITES

204. The Best Sous Vide Eggs
(Ready in about 1 hour 20 minutes | Servings 4)

Are you ready for a healthy and satisfying breakfast? Sous vide eggs are fancy, sophisticated, and delicious.
Per serving: 360 Calories; 26.6g Fat; 9.2g Carbs; 22.4g Protein; 2.6g Sugars

Ingredients

4 eggs

1 tablespoon olive oil

2 garlic cloves

2 tablespoons scallions, chopped

2 tomatoes, sliced

10 ounces spinach, tough stems discarded

1/2 teaspoon salt

1/4 teaspoon freshly ground pepper

Directions

- Preheat a sous vide water bath to 150 degrees F.
- Now, cook your eggs for 1 hour 15 minutes.
- Meanwhile, heat olive oil in a skillet over a medium-high heat. Cook the garlic and scallions until aromatic. Add tomatoes and cook an additional 3 minutes.
- Stir in spinach; stir until it is wilted. Season with salt and pepper and serve with sous vide eggs. Bon appétit!

---

205. Spicy Omelet with Romano Cheese
(Ready in about 20 minutes | Servings 3)

Serve this protein-packed, piquant omelet and delight your family. You can mix it up with whatever you have on hand – leeks, pepper, mushrooms or cream cheese.
Per serving: 427 Calories; 33.7g Fat; 6.4g Carbs; 22.9g Protein; 3.2g Sugars

Ingredients

6 eggs, whisked

1 red onion, chopped

1/2 teaspoon garlic paste

1 jalapeno pepper, chopped

2 tablespoons butter

1/2 cup Romano cheese, grated

Salt, to taste

1/2 teaspoon ground black pepper

1/4 cup fresh cilantro, chopped

Directions

- Preheat a sous vide water bath to 160 degrees F.
- Mix the eggs with onion, garlic paste, jalapeno, butter, cheese, salt, and ground black pepper.
- Pour the egg mixture into cooking pouches; seal tightly. Submerge the cooking pouches in the water bath; cook for 15 minutes.
- Divide the omelet among serving plates and serve garnished with fresh cilantro. Bon appétit!

206. Quinoa with Dried Fruits and Walnuts
(Ready in about 7 hours | Servings 6)

If you've never tried an overnight quinoa, keep an open mind. With sous vide cooking, quinoa becomes juicy, fluffy and infused with the delicious flavors of spices, dried fruits and nuts. Enjoy!

Per serving: 506 Calories; 9.6g Fat; 93.7g Carbs; 14.2g Protein; 19.7g Sugars

Ingredients

1 ½ cups quinoa, rinsed
3 ½ cups rice milk
1/2 teaspoon ground cinnamon
1/4 teaspoon grated nutmeg
1/4 teaspoon kosher salt

1 teaspoon vanilla paste
1/3 cup sugar
1 cup dried prunes, pitted and chopped
1/2 cup golden raisins
1/2 cup walnuts, chopped

Directions

- Preheat a sous vide water bath to 176 degrees F.
- Place all ingredients in cooking pouches; seal tightly. Submerge the cooking pouches in the water bath; cook for 7 hours.
- Serve with some extra milk, shredded coconut or fresh fruit. Bon appétit!

207. Vanilla and Lemon Syrup
(Ready in about 1 hour 20 minutes | Servings 10)

Here's a homemade pancake syrup your family will love. If you like lemon cookies, then you'll love this buttery syrup. Perfect for stacked pancakes or homemade waffles.

Per serving: 164 Calories; 9.2g Fat; 21.3g Carbs; 0.1g Protein; 19.4g Sugars

Ingredients

1 stick butter, at room temperature
1 cup maple syrup
1 teaspoon vanilla paste
A pinch of grated nutmeg
A pinch of ground star anise

1 tablespoon lemon juice
1 tablespoon lemon peel, grated
1/4 teaspoon grated ginger
1/4 teaspoon table salt

Directions

- Preheat a sous vide water bath to 140 degrees F.
- Simply put all of the above ingredients into a cooking pouch; seal tightly. Submerge the cooking pouch in the water bath; cook for 1 hour 15 minutes.
- Serve immediately or refrigerate for up to 2 weeks. Bon appétit!

208. Hearty Pumpkin Risotto
(Ready in about 1 hour | Servings 6)

We've adapted this autumn classic recipe and cook it in a sous vide water bath. It turns out great!
Per serving: 225 Calories; 2.9g Fat; 41.3g Carbs; 7.3g Protein; 1.3g Sugars

Ingredients

1 ½ cups white rice

2 cups pumpkin, diced

2 teaspoons coconut oil

1/4 cup scallions, chopped

4 ½ cups broth, preferably homemade

2 sprigs fresh thyme, chopped

1/4 teaspoon ground black pepper

1/2 teaspoon cayenne pepper

Salt, to taste

A small handful of coriander, roughly chopped

Directions

- Preheat a sous vide water bath to 183 degrees F.
- Then, simply place all ingredients, except the coriander, in a large-sized cooking pouch; seal tightly. Submerge the cooking pouch in the water bath; cook for 50 minutes.
- Spoon the risotto into individual bowls; serve garnished with chopped coriander. Bon appétit!

---

209. Mom's Candied Yams
(Ready in about 2 hours 15 minutes | Servings 6)

These candied yams are made with the magic of sous vide cooking, which enriches flavors and makes the whole process fun and easy.
Per serving: 225 Calories; 2.9g Fat; 41.3g Carbs; 7.3g Protein; 1.3g Sugars

Ingredients

2 ½ pounds yams, peeled and sliced

1 cup butter, unsalted

1/2 cup dark brown sugar, packed

1 orange, juice and zest

1 ¼ cups pecans, roughly chopped

1/4 teaspoon ground ginger

1 teaspoon cinnamon

1 teaspoon vanilla extract

1/2 teaspoon almond extract

A pinch of salt

A pinch of grated nutmeg

Directions

- Preheat a sous vide water bath to 160 degrees F.
- Place yams in cooking pouches; seal tightly. Submerge the cooking pouch in the water bath; cook for 1 hour 45 minutes.
- Remove yams from the cooking pouch and pat dry.
- Preheat your oven to 360 degrees F. Place yams on a parchment-lined baking sheet.
- In a pan, bring butter, sugar, orange, pecans, ginger, cinnamon, vanilla and almond extract, salt, and nutmeg to a boil. Now, remove from heat and pour this syrup over sous vide yams.
- Bake in the preheated oven for 25 minutes. Enjoy!

210. Frittata Di Zucchine
(Ready in about 30 minutes | Servings 4)

Eggs cook wonderfully in a sous vide water bath. They are cooked all the way through, and, best of all, they have great, silky texture and deep flavor.

Per serving: 355 Calories; 25.2g Fat; 9g Carbs; 24.8g Protein; 1.4g Sugars

Ingredients

2 teaspoons olive oil

1 ½ pounds zucchini, sliced

1 shallot, chopped

2 garlic cloves, minced

6 eggs, beaten

3 ounces Ricotta cheese, at room temperature

1/2 teaspoon ground sage

1 tablespoon dried chervil

1/4 teaspoon dried marjoram

1/2 teaspoon dried savory

1/4 teaspoon yellow mustard

1/4 teaspoon ground black pepper

Sea salt, to taste

1/2 cup Romano cheese, shredded

Directions

- Preheat a sous vide water bath to 170 degrees F.
- Heat olive oil in a nonstick pan that is preheated over a moderately high heat. Once hot, sauté the zucchini, shallot, and garlic until softened.
- Transfer the sautéed vegetables to cooking pouches. Add the eggs, Ricotta, and spices; seal tightly. Submerge the cooking pouch in the water bath; cook for 25 minutes.
- Transfer to a lightly greased baking dish. Top with cheese and bake at 370 degrees F until the cheese is completely melted.
- Serve in individual plates, garnished with pickles. Bon appétit!

---

211. Easy Homemade Cheese
(Ready in about 1 hour 50 minutes | Servings 10)

An easy and flavorful homemade cheese is a gourmet's dream. It is worth the effort especially if you have access to a good-quality, organic milk.

Per serving: 220 Calories; 10.4g Fat; 25.6g Carbs; 6g Protein; 25.4g Sugars

Ingredients

8 cups whole milk

1 cup heavy cream

4 ounces distilled white vinegar

1/2 teaspoon citric acid

1 teaspoon salt

Directions

- Preheat a sous vide water bath to 170 degrees F.
- Pour the milk and heavy cream into a large cooking pouch; seal tightly. Submerge the cooking pouch in the water bath; cook for 35 minutes.
- Now, add the vinegar, citric acid, and salt; cook for a further 13 minutes more.
- Place the curd in a colander, lined with a few layers of cheesecloth; allow it to sit for 1 hour. Bon appétit!

212. Saucy Peppery Risotto
(Ready in about 3 hours 35 minutes | Servings 4)

Light, saucy and spicy, this risotto would win your heart. If you don't like a spicy food, just skip serrano pepper.
Per serving: 385 Calories; 11.4g Fat; 60.3g Carbs; 10.5g Protein; 3.6g Sugars

Ingredients

2 tablespoons butter
1 yellow onion, chopped
2 garlic cloves, smashed
2 bell peppers, deseeded and chopped
1 serrano pepper, deseeded and chopped

Sea salt and ground black pepper, to taste
1 ½ cups brown rice, rinsed
1 bay leaf
3 cups broth, preferably homemade
1/2 cup fresh parsley, roughly chopped

Directions

- Preheat a sous vide water bath to 183 degrees F.
- In a sauté pan, melt the butter over moderate heat. Now, sauté the onion, garlic, and peppers until softened; season with salt and black pepper.
- Transfer the sautéed mixture to a large-sized cooking pouch. Add brown rice, bay leaf, and broth; seal tightly. Submerge the cooking pouch in the water bath; cook for 3 hours 30 minutes.
- Taste, adjust the seasonings and divide your risotto among serving bowls. Serve garnished with fresh parsley. Bon appétit!

213. Calabrian-Style Pasta Sauce
(Ready in about 40 minutes | Servings 8)

The only thing better than a jarred pasta sauce is a sous vide pasta sauce! Try your ultimate comfort food in a completely new way.
Per serving: 51 Calories; 0.7g Fat; 11.3g Carbs; 2.2g Protein; 7.5g Sugars

Ingredients

2 (28-ounce) cans whole tomatoes
1/2 fennel bulb, chopped
1 teaspoon Calabrian chili paste
1/2 teaspoon cayenne pepper
1/2 teaspoon paprika
4 cloves garlic, minced
1 tablespoon dried basil

1 tablespoon dried oregano
1 teaspoon dried rosemary
1/2 teaspoon dried thyme
1/4 teaspoon black pepper, preferably freshly ground
1 tablespoon sugar
Salt, to taste

Directions

- Preheat a sous vide water bath to 190 degrees F.
- Add all of the above ingredients to a large cooking pouch; seal tightly. Submerge the cooking pouch in the water bath; cook for 35 minutes.
- You can use your sauce immediately or store in the freezer. Use a sous vide water bath to thaw frozen sauce at 130 degrees F. Bon appétit!

214. Honeydew Melon with Mint-Orange Syrup
(Ready in about 1 hour 50 minutes | Servings 8)

The ultimate in freshness, this syrup works great with lemonade, desserts, whipped cream, and so on.
Per serving: 136 Calories; 0g Fat; 34.6g Carbs; 0.2g Protein; 33.1g Sugars

Ingredients

1/2 pound oranges, sliced

2 ½ cups superfine sugar

2 cups water

1 tablespoon fresh mint leaves, thinly sliced

1/2 teaspoon cloves

1 honeydew melon, seeded

Directions

- Preheat a sous vide water bath to 140 degrees F.
- Place sliced oranges, sugar, water, mint and cloves in a large-sized cooking pouch; seal tightly. Submerge the cooking pouch in the water bath; cook for 1 hour 45 minutes.
- Allow your syrup to cool completely; then, place in the refrigerator until ready to serve.
- In the meantime, scoop out melon into balls using a melon baller; place in a serving bowl.
- Strain the cooking liquid through a sieve. To serve, toss melon balls with cooled syrup.
- You can store this syrup in refrigerator for up to 4 weeks. Enjoy!

---

215. Homemade Rum Cocktail
(Ready in about 35 minutes | Servings 2)

Here is a great reason for whipping up a batch of ginger syrup! Homemade rum cocktail! This sous vide ginger syrup really shines in this cocktail.
Per serving: 163 Calories; 5.2g Fat; 17.9g Carbs; 11.6g Protein; 14.8g Sugars

Ingredients

1/4 cup fresh ginger, grated

1/4 cup brown sugar, packed

1/4 cup water

4 ounces dark rum

2 ounces fresh orange juice

4 ounces soda water

Directions

- Preheat a sous vide water bath to 183 degrees F.
- To make a ginger syrup, place fresh ginger, brown sugar, and 1/4 cup of water in a cooking pouch; seal tightly. Submerge the cooking pouch in the water bath; cook for 25 minutes.
- Combine ginger syrup with dark rum and orange juice in a cocktail shaker; fill the shaker with ice, and shake about 15 seconds.
- Add soda water and serve well-chilled. Enjoy!

27399377R00072

Made in the USA
Lexington, KY
29 December 2018